Lyn Lifshin

A Critical Study

by

Hugh Fox

The Whitston Publishing Company
Troy, New York
1985

Copyright 1985
Hugh Fox

Library of Congress Catalog Card Number 84-52092

ISBN 0-87875-299-4

Printed in the United States of America

Women's Center
206 Washington Street
Blacksburg, VA 24061-0270
(540) 231-7806

Lyn Lifshin

For Menke Katz—For the

View from Inside the Mandala.

INTRODUCTION

Lyn Lifshin is both the most widely published and most widely misunderstood poet on the scene today. Of course to a certain extent the misunderstanding is Lifshin's own fault because when she appeared on the scene in the sixties the image she projected was that of a blonde, vamp rock-star type, all juice and high voltage, when in fact she was a suburban housewife who had finished 90% of the work on a Ph.D. in English—so you might even call her scholarly. In fact she was and remains, like one of her spiritual ancestors, Emily Dickinson, somewhat of a recluse, shy, introverted, obsessed with diet and exercise, radiating an aura of high intellectuality and comprehensive understanding of herself and her surrounding world. I guess the concept I'm reaching for is that of "detachment," *being in the world but not part of it.*

In a sense her emergence as a poet grew out of her being flunked out of the Ph.D. program at SUNY-Albany. As we'll see the flunking-out process was cruel, chauvinistic, arbitrary; and it was the first time in a brilliant, quick academic ascent that she ever had met failure. Her reaction was to turn against academe and identify herself with the most radical, anti-academic poets of the 60's, namely the so-called Meat School headed up by the arch-iconoclast, our Van Gogh, our Rimbaud, our *Bete Noir, Poet Maudit,* Charles Bukowski.

Bukowski's purpose as a writer was to totally step outside the academic, the "conventional," the "literary," and write poetry that smacked of the street, the racetrack, the brothel, poetry that was totally honest, as "formless" as possible—although with always a deft sense of diction/word-choice. And that was the model that Lifshin chose for herself.

You'd see her picture on every book, long blonde straggly hair and heavily mascared eyes, staring out like the quintessential Vamp, tough, at the same time delicate, naive, at the same time full of street-wisdom.

She submitted everywhere. She made a campaign, a crusade, out of appearing in every magazine that came out. And if she didn't get accepted at first try she'd drown the editor with batch after batch of submissions until she finally made it in. I remember as editor of GHOST DANCE getting the Lifshin treatment; and finally I found something I really liked . . . she appeared.

Only this kind of saturation bombing also had its negative effects. She left herself at the mercy of editors and to a great extent the type of poetry that got accepted was superficial, tough-gal poems about Lifshin as Vamp in action. This is what I mean by being misunderstood. The Lifshin image that everyone accepted really had nothing to do with Lifshin, and when her serious poetry began to come out in the seventies it was largely bypassed in favor of Lifshin as "rock-star." So that while she was in fact producing one of the most impressive bodies of work in American literature, the old image stuck—Lifshin in the popular imagination remained a "Bukowskian."

What was actually happening during the seventies was that Lifshin had begun a series of what might be termed time-travel books in which she had completely abandoned any identification with Bukowski and was indirectly searching for her roots in all possible American pasts. Lifshin was, in fact, a Jew who had been alienated from her Jewishness and was now on a quest to refind spiritual roots/origins. She'd go to Plymouth, to the old house up on the Hudson, project herself back into colonial times and ask herself "What does this American past have to do with me?" With the inevitable answer coming back at her—nothing. She went to England and tried the same time-projection technique There. Again nothing. But then in the American southwest (and among the Eskimos) she began to find spiritual rapport and found in Amerindia a spiritual reality that was homologous to the spiritual reality that she had suppressed in her own personal life. What most impressed her about the Amerindian past, from South America all the way to the North Pole, was not merely its sense of ordered sacredness, but its ability to overlay and encrust the sacred with sensual richness. It wasn't the thin, watered-down spirituality of white America, but a heavy, sensuous spirituality that approached her own lost Jewish past. And in the course of this discovery she wrote some of the profoundest poetry ever written about the American Indian, not written as an observer at all, but a participant in the Indian mystique/"Way."

She also began to write extensively about her own lost religious past. The quests were simultaneous—to find herself in herself and also in Amerindia. These "lost-and-found Jewishness" poems, of course, are another important document in their own way, a Jewish equivalent of ROOTS, and one of the most telling series of poems ever written about alienation from origins, from one's own personal-historical past.

More recently Lifshin has done an anthology centering on the relationship between daughter and mother and another anthology of women's diaries—both from major "commercial" presses. You can almost predict, in fact, that her next step will be into the commercial mainstream—the way of Marge Piercy, Anne Sexton, Joyce Carol Oates.

Special Lifshin issues of magazines like POETRY NOW, THE GREENFIELD REVIEW and STONEY HILLS have come out recently, and nowadays she writes regularly for ROLLING STONE; she's on the brink of poetic stardom, with all of its potential perils so intimately interlaced with its rewards.

What I've tried to do in this volume is chart out the voyage of the poet from early beginnings up to this moment of "going commercial." Maybe the book is even written for Lifshin herself so she has a chart of where she's been to better enable her to make sense out of where she's going—and what she should avoid.

The quotes are copious on purpose because most of the books I'm quoting from are out of print and I want the reader to get as full a feeling for the work itself as possible, Lifshin herself has helped me in writing the book. She's read and commented on the manuscript, and what I may have missed during direct interview she has supplied in subsequent letters. At the same time she's resisted an impulse to totally re-write the book; after all it is a view from the outside, not autobiography.

I think this is exactly the right time for this book to appear. Criticism should be written by the contemporaries of the poets so it is based not on some distant, scholarly reading of a printed text but also incorporates a feeling for the reality of the living person, the voice, "tone," whole projected personality.

The centuries pass quickly. To anyone reading these words in some distant future, let me assure you that they were written not merely from a personal acquaintanceship with the poet but also from having lived, along with her, through the same heady years of the sixties, the stalemate years of the seventies, and into the depression years of the eighties. We were young together, we aged together; in a sense much of what I say about Lifshin I could just as well be saying about myself . . . or the "ages" through which we lived.

E. Lansing, 1983

CHAPTER I

When Lyn Lifshin emerges onto the literary scene with WHY IS THE HOUSE DISSOLVING? in 1968, she sounds like a female Bukowski, tough, with an iconoclastic wallop that leaves you a bit off balance:

> She going to town
> legs shaved way up
> to see if he knocked her
> up doctor say press legs apart
> on the table with white towel
> covering cunt, metal prong scratching
> inside slit cold she think
> and he pressing her belly,
> then looking at juice
> he says not to worry.
> And as she trots home
> blood warmly in her nylon crotch
> she sigh happy
> red shining sticky down her leg.
> (Edited and printed by Brown Miller,
> *Open Skull Press*, San Francisco, no pagination)

Even the "She going" instead of "she goes," the "doctor say" instead of "doctor says" . . . she's creating the image of herself as, what, immigrant, the *most* inner-city transported-from-the-rural-South-black, Latina. . . .? "Knocked up," "cunt," "juice" . . . it's really unprecedented isn't it? Even someone like THE daring Sharon Asselin in BACK TO EARTH tempered vaginal reality with a certain porcelain "femininity." But here it's back up against the wall of Hard Reality, The Spirit of Buk reincarnated as Mother Night.
Level 1.
Level 2 . . . we walk into the Lifshin World of dissolving surrealism:

> Lace grows in her eyes like
> fat weddings....
>> ("Waiting, the Hallways Under Her
>> Skin Thick with Dreamchildren.")

> "Behind walls
> he waits with a
> bomb in his head...."
>> ("At This Place")

> Her fingers are weaving
> veins of small insects.
>> ("And for Once")

> A girl is growing on canvas.
> In the middle of becoming
> a map of seasons
> breaks out from her thigh,
> horses of wood and hair struggling
> in back of old dreams.
>> ("Studio 1")

Bukowski and the "Meatists"/Meat School were also into surrealism at this same, at this culminating moment of a decade of experimental American Language-outreaching, but there's a difference here between, say, the still-awkward often self-cancelling-out surrealistics of a Blazek or a Bukowski, and Lifshin's "true"-surrealism, not adopting the surreal as an adjunct to a tough-guy essentially realistic vision of the world, but starting from inside, fermenting within a Bretonesque night of the soul, and then allowing herself to "bubble-out" into visibility. As Brown Miller points out in his April 1968, introduction to Blazek's ALL GODS MUST LEARN TO KILL (Analecta Press, 1968):

> Douglas Blazek refuses to escape from life through poetry; instead he uses poetry as an incredibly insistent hollow drill with which he can tunnel his way deep into the most forbidding experiences.... All artists readily embrace the imagination, the main muse, but Blazek uses imaginative thought to go in a direction quite opposite to that of most creative people; he clears away the artifice and decorative parts of perception and gives the render a

crisp and devastating view of the way the universe really is. . . .

As if "most" creative artists are somehow bogged down in "artifice" and "decoration"!?! But . . . the idea of "direction" is important here. Blazek *is* tunnelling from outside in. It's only in the mid-sixties that he reaches that quiet mind-place where Lifshin is (really!) starting out from. Her surrealistic trajectory *is* from the inside out. The clairvoyant later Lifshin is already here, even if slightly covered by "stance" and "posture":

> Snow on your hair,
> the room so warm and
> everything melting,
> there we thought of
> starting but it was all
> over, that's the way
> it had to stay. Dust
> in our throats, the same
> dried flowers on the wall
> and we leaving half relieved,
> clutching iced branches,
> glad for the cold.
>
> ("That February")

The real "trick" here is that she is able to carry off the "stance"/"posture" at all, create at all this world of "urinegrey snow" where the wind licks "raw bones" where the end-of-the-sixties air is "full of/colonels who love/killing some enemy," and the Veteran's Day streets are filled with "sandals strewn with/ribbons of flesh."[1] Because the fact is that WHY IS THE HOUSE DISSOLVING? does *not* emerge from experiences parallel with those of Blazek, Brown Miller, Sharon Asselin, Richmond or Bukowski, that whole West Coast vortex that was right in the middle of the simultaneous protest and quest experience that capped the decade, and Lifshin was a suburban housewife who had just flunked her Ph.D. orals, who had been on the brink of writing a Ph.D. dissertation and disappearing (alternative route: Lifshin as academic!) into academe.

She has a number of poems about *her* 60's (in contrast to the west coast sixties of Be-Ins, Love-Ins, the Free Speech Movement, Dirty Speech Movement, the whole centrifugal

Berkeley hysteria that culminates in the Big Nixon Freeze), like "You Understand the Requirements"—"about the notification that she's flunked her orals":

> We are
> sorry to have to
> regret to
> tell you
> regret sorry that you have
> failed
>
> your hair should have been
> piled up higher
>
> you have failed to
> pass failed
> your sorry
> regret your
> final hair comprehensive
> exam satisfactorily. . . .[2]

You can't call this "feminist," really, it's not part of any platform or crusade, but the sense of the Female Squelched is strong, the anger hot. In another poem, "Orals," she creates a Daumier-like sketch of the all-male board that flunked her. She comes in, one of the professors asks her what she thinks about adultery, another says she reminds him of Theda Bara, and then one of them:

> . . . scratches on ear and wants
> to know if tottel's 3rd
> cousin by a later
> marriage of course
> is significant in 19th
> century bibliography and
> my god he is serious I
> sweat inside my specially
> lengthened drab gray suit. . . .[3]

In a way, of course, this rejection by the academic establishment is a parallel experience to the rejection-experiences (rejecting *and* being rejected) of the West Coast Meat School, a more subtle but no less painful variation of general sixties Outsiderism.

This rejection, in fact, becomes a pivotal psychological point in Lifshin's whole later development. As she told me in December of 1980:

> ... I was so angry at the academic world when I left that I wanted to be nothing like them. I wouldn't even publish in a magazine that was connected with a college at that time. I wanted to publish in magazines like Blazek's OLE, Steve Richmond's EARTH ... just the real "meat" kind of magazines....[4]

When she wrote her Statement of Literary Purpose for Number 10 of Carol Berge's CENTER she hit back again on the same burning point:

> ... I know I wanted more than anything to write but was scared ... and I let things like graduate school and even painting get in the way. Anger was what finally broke thru the let-me-wait-a-little wall of delay, mainly at one man who was the reason I didn't go and write (I should dedicate a book to him) scholarly articles instead of what I really wanted to do. After a near Ph.D. and then not getting it, I thot I'll show that prick I'll do what he probably wanted to and didn't. The most anthologized poem of mine, "You Understand the Requiements," came from that experience and I feel many of my good poems are anger poems....[5]

This violent shifting away from the academic is *so* important because it prevents once and for all the development of that *other* Lifshin who may very well have contracted the disease that infects almost all university-supported contemporary U. S. poets and that in retrospect will be seen as the most single nefarious influence on U. S. poetry in the second half of the twentieth-century, namely Academic Isolationistis, Acute Cuteness, Crafty-Artiness, Ashberyia. From WHY IS THE HOUSE DISSOLVING? on Lifshin retains a "plain" honesty that keeps open the channels between Self and Public. She's not "masked" or a "poser" and in fact in that same CENTER statement she goes on to make a kind of poetic Declaration of Poetic Intent that shows just how intimately honest her poetry was/is:

> ... many poems seem to come before the experience they relate. More than most people would guess. WHY IS THE HOUSE DISSOLVING? knew more about how my house-walls were falling apart then than I did. . . .[6]

The house is dissolving because it doesn't allow her any room to grow. "Yes, this is our house," she says, "but it's hard to/remember, do we really live here? We have doors and garages but/where are we growing, where/are our windows, have we any real shelter?"[7]

And the poems themselves serve as a kind of "scouting-party" to reconnoiter the psychic-territory she'll later occupy. At this early stage, Lifshin is like a inchoate wandering spirit looking for an identity to inhabit, and her "concretization" in the form of Meat Poet—in spite of her own vision of WHY IS THE HOUSE DISSOLVING?—is really just a small fraction of the whole.

She is successful in "concretizing" as Meat Poet, the rhythms ring nicely in a poem like "Not Quite Spring" ("Baby you know I get high/on you, come back with me/whispering in her car . . ."), the pink-light humor's fun in a poem like "Chewing up the Sun" with its plumber and his "pink, tipped/plunger thickly flaring/from a swollen bag," but the existential heart of the book is in poems that on one hand neither talk about her mad housewife diarist ("The Way Sun Keeps Falling Away From Every Window") *nor* take on the street-stance of a Blazek or Bukowski, the ambiguous confusing poems like the three Studio poems that lay down the outline for her whole future career as FLOATING UNCERTAIN EXISTENTIALIST LOOKING FOR A FORM SHE CAN BE COMFORTABLE WITH . . . AND WHICH—INCIDENTALLY—SHE NEVER FINDS.

Already in "Studio 1" you find the dead-ancestral-voice image that becomes a thematic mainstay throughout her work. A girl *is* "gorwing on canvas," but the growing is interferred with by a process of ancestral-identity-seeking that refuses to leave her:

> But the lost bones that keep
> calling for names—
> as if an old story had

> entered their blood
> with no end, no
> beginning—
>
> never leave her, stay always,
> unanswered
>
> forever.

In a sense she sees herself disenabled from ever entering totally into the Now, participating in any sort of "groupness," fellow-feeling, camaraderie. The Power ("the girl with a/city of leaves in her thigh") is already there in Studio 2, but—echoes of Eliot's HOLLOW MEN—unable to ever "realize" itself:

> . . . the girl with a
> city of leaves
> in her thigh
>
> where they will stay
> like trapped stars
> or poems
> lost and
> saved
>
> forever,

which is a curious double-entendre that shows subjective emotion/feeling/impulse cut off from social participation (lost) but at the same time "saved" as art/expression, "frozen." We *are* the hollow men/women and "here in back of/old wood glass//only thistles and feathers/grow from the pale/skulls of mice."

In "Studio 3" there's the very revealing image of Lifshin so to speak "between worlds," struggling toward inclusion in The Human Family (Meat, or Suburban, or Academic, or . . .) but never able to shift out of the vacuum of permanent inter-space:

> terror
> emerges is
> floating over the wheat,
> over a city of thighs
> and she falls

> stumbling toward love
> somewhere between two places
> that she has forgotten
> how to name
> or remember
> like a dream she has known
> and does not

"Stumbling toward love/somewhere between two places/that she has forgotten how to name. . . ." Here is the leitmotif for all the later poetry . . . the puse/impulse/drive toward "love" (defined as "inclusion within any sort of group-plasma) between two places which may be defined as poles of uncertainty/non-definition/non-identity.

The "Jewishness" is an important factor here:

> . . . I think we were all sort of looked at as being weird because we were Jewish. I was always kind of peculiar. . . .[8]

Growing up Lifshin lives in a Gentile world, Jewish, but not "really," lacking community/contextual support, feeling excluded from full "Jewishness," at the same time never really being "gentile" either: "once when i was/walking home from/school the elastic/on my underpants died/The next day someone/wrote kike on the/blackboard/both i knew were simply a result of fat."[9]

Lifshin has a "complex" about thinness. She keeps herself wraithlike, semi-starved, and here, I think, is the key to her obsession desire to "minimalize" herself as well as her almost total lack of group identification. In fact don't the two go together? She isn't inventing her "outsiderness," she is de facto the classic L'Estranger, sociologically outside (she even remembers, remarks on the fact that she lived in the only apartment building in a town of houses) of all "groups," keeping herself "small" (read "thin") in order to almost disappear, intellectually brilliant (and beautiful) but being "punished" on both accounts with Mind being rejected because of Body (the whole Ph.D. Whipping-experience) and Body wanting to self-destruct because of the rejection of Mind. So minimizing "body" altogether—in spite of these "sex-projections" in the early work that are defensive, screening, clouding reactions—what we have in 1968, at the very outset of The Career, is a kind of disembodied "esprit" looking for path/face/identity. The first "embodiment" here in WHY IS

THE HOUSE DISSOLVING?, for all its partialness, is that of Lifshin as Meat Poet. In successive "embodiments" Lifshin leaves the contemporary altogether, moves through the American Past, into old houses and personalities, haunting derelict worlds for fragments/traces of a past that she doesn't have but must reconstruct. Her whole career, then, becomes a series of small quests; she remains quicksilverishly not undefined but constantly re-self-defining, and a study of her work must be as quick in pursuit of masks/defenses/"poses" a she is in assuming them. Certainly in WHY IS THE HOUSE DISSOLVING? the only "essential Lifshin" under the attempt to taking an identifying stance with her contemporaries, is Lifshin "stumbling toward love/somewhere between two places/that she has forgotten how to name. . . ."

After all she saw herself at the time of the writing of WHY IS THE HOUSE DISSOLVING? as a kind of prisoner of the bourgeoisie, caged in an overprotective, loveless marriage that in itself was *an* identity that she was to soon abandon for a real initiation of pilgrimage:

> . . . in my life, in my real life, my life was so subdued and so isolated and so . . . I was living almost like a nun really . . . it was so secluded, protected. . . .[10]

So that WHY IS THE HOUSE DISSOLVING? *is* a dissolving of old frames and references, and her prophetic vision that the work is the vanguard of the life begins to fulfill itself, her "real" (real imagination) life beginning its movement toward her REAL (read Existential) life.

NOTES

[1] "Albany Night," and "Dark Sun."
[2] In OFFERED BY OWNER, Natalie Slohm Associates Inc., 1978, p. 9.
[3] *Ibid.*, pp. 11-14.
[4] Interview, Schenectady, December 11, 1980.

[5] CENTER, #10, p. 20, ed. Carol Berge, address given in issue, where Berge would be teaching the following year (University of Southern Mississippi in Hattiesburg). The point of the issue was to give contributors a chance to air their views on work, life, vision of art, perceptions, etc.
[6] CENTER, #10, p. 20.
[7] Title poem, WHY IS THE HOUSE DISSOLVING?.
[8] From December 11, 1980 interview.
[9] In OFFERED BY OWNER, pp. 16-22.
[10] From December 11, 1980 interview.

CHAPTER II

LEAVES AND NIGHT THINGS (Baby John Press, 1970) in a sense is a Self-Portrait of Lifshin as Self-annihilator. Not "suicide," but a total suppression, dissolving, atomization of Self, the next logical step after the process of "breaking away" implied in her 1968 volume WHY IS THE HOUSE DISSOLVING? The accent here isn't on the "why" but the "dissolving." In a way she carries over a faded Meat Poet image/technique from WHY IS THE HOUSE DISSOLVING?, but goes one step further into the Kamakazi-death that precedes the samurai-resurrection.

There are the sexual-frustration-overtone poems like "office" with its horny secretaries at work, the perfect picture of essential, sexual woman subordinated to the trivial asexualities of office work:

> ... morning sets in, perfumed wool and sweat rising to a soft mist high over the desks and the grey duplicating machines.[1]

There's the obvious connecting line drawn between ballet and "blocked" sex:

> ... everybody said her
> pointes weren't bad
> and her tutu
> so pretty,
> love or marriage
> out for now
> so disciplined was she,
> days off she let her boyfriend
> rub his fingers up her thigh.[2]

There's even one poem on John B. Stetson that's a beautifully wrought piece of objective social-history that's a wry comment on the Darwinistic-Industrial "saw" that work is health/

salvation. Stetson's T. B. is cured by his business success: "Some of the hats lasted/15 years, or 20/John B. Stetson lasted for 76."[3]

The dominant "mood"/"image"/"thrust" of the book, though, isn't anything sunlit and dialogueable, but an almost mute plunging into the primordia of the Unconscious, the sea of primal death-wish reality that serves as a self-cancelling device to allow the poet rebirth in other forms.

One form of this psychic landscape is Total Freeze:

> A skinny moon that is hardly
> The snow ragged swamp trees.
>
> Bones of remembered faces
> are blown white in winter
> alphabets. Snow lips
>
> Cranberry lips. A vision of
> sailors' lips knocking at
>
> sea rock and stubble.
> And the coldest sea ever.
>
> Fish wreathed in ice
> gleam.[4]

Lifshin herself, of course, is the "skinny moon" that *is* "hardly" (i.e. hardly exists). And *as* moon/moon-goddess—Ruler of Subconscious Night—she enters into a world of psychic-swamps that are (identity-suspension) ragged with snow. Memory is obliterated ("remembered faces/are blown white") in the transmuting code of self-as-it-now-exists negation ("in winter alphabets"). Is the vision of the sailors' lips "knocking at/sea rock and stubble" an ancestral intrusion of some kind, the sea a rite of passage from a previous (Jewish? Old World?) life now be reasserted from deep inside her identity lacking inner-sea?

The poem ends interestingly enough with "miraculous turtles" blooming in the "dreams of the/high school science teacher" (Spring,/the voice of the turtle/Imagination invading Lifshin herself as arch 'Suburban rationalist') and an image is tagged on at the end of "the wind full of so many/night horses and no riders."

At times the psychic landscape goes through a kind of cyclic death-rebirth, depressive-low followed by manic high. Like "Leaning Over the Bridge at Otter Creek." It's spring, the freeze is over, she stands watching "winter dripping slow/from the gargoyles" (Gothic interior "horrors," the tortured encapsulated self, more historically-oriented alternative version of The Unconscious), there's a whirlpool (transition-state/release-,/change-factor) in front of her, and she looks for "something/of that strange girl/who leaped into the/breaking up snow//that distant spring/when faces sneered/the water pulled her,"[5] which is a projection out of Lifshin's own stasis into a surrogate suicide-victim who—like herself—felt (or at least she imagines she felt) sneered at, "outsidered," rejected by the American "clan."

Interestingly enough, though, the speculation here doesn't stop at the projection into somebody else's suicide, the fastening on to another (again surrogate) scapegoated "victim," but moves into a very positive easterlike resurrection-image:

> watch for her shadow
> to come floating
> high over the chestnut
> trees and the church
>
> spire blurred in the
> distance.

And the "Listen/for March to/break in the water"? Thaw, spring, cyclic rebirth . . . the victim reincarnates as The Spirit of Renewal, Lifshin visualizing herself as 1). Rejected, annihilated, destroyed, then 2). Re-emerging in another (manic) form. BUT the massacre is necessary. This is the repeated theme. The goat (Self A) must be sacrificed to asure the renewal of the world (all multiples of future selves).

In "Going Under," there's almost an "accomodation" to a permanent state of "drowning"/"suffociation"/"rootlessness." To the establishmentarian Lifshin sees that her between-world state may seem totally unacceptable/destructive:

> Well yes, there were
> claws and scales
> underwater
> teeth and worse

> but not just
> sea beasts,
> it may seem that way
> to you
> all those
> words and shells
> surfacing.....

To the "reader," she's saying, her work ("words and shells") may give the *impression* of some sort of undersea/subconscious process of self-mutilation and *angst*, but for her, seeing the *angst*-world from inside, the World of The Beast, through the Eyes of the Beast, it was a much more positive vision; "fish and water-flowers/twisted toward me/it was alright, really/treading weeds/loose as the sea's loose." In other words the whole process of psychic unloosing in her work, filled her with a kind of exuberance, an affaltus of liberation; it would have been much worse without the escapehatch of The Word, itself. Although even with all this orthopsychological "releasing," there is the problem of love-isolation/aloneness:

> thinking of you
> on some land
> I couldn't get to.

Lifshin's whole attitude toward her "free" aloneness is complexly ambiguous. On one hand there's the freedom of the voyager into the solitary depths of the liberated unconsciousness, but on the other the return of the deep need to "make-contact," keep a link with The Conscious/The Affective/The "Normative."

"Please," for example, begins with an image of love in a peaceful garage (ground-/conscious-level), then moves into the celler, but even here not an ordinary cellar, a cellar below everything (totally out of conscious "sight"):

> ... the
> celler's darker
> we'll go
> down under
> everything......

Then, unexpectedly, once inside the this nest of the unconscious, instead of any sort of expected "solace,"/sanctuary/relief, the poet finds herself alone again, returning to the state of buried (or drowned) alienation:

> Later we could
> be in that
> close damp
> listening for
> spiders. Only
> hurry, I'm in too
> deep to stay
> without you.

She's gotten to some sort of psychic-burrowing record here hasn't she, beyond tolerance, limit, to the outermost (innermost) point of existential stress. She's breaking away into new depths of Self, then gets to the end of her tether, to the point of "breaking," and wants, if not back, then at least company.

There's even one poem reminiscent of Eliot's Prufrockian[6] claws, in which Lifshin longs for psychic-paralysis. Like a potato ("I'd/rather stay numb/and dusty, like/potatoes . . .") and all the time quite aware that this dusty numbness has become at least temporarily a pattern in her work: ". . . tho I'm/ wondering if they/should be in this/poem, lately they/seem to be in so/ many others. . . ."[7]

Throughout LEAVES AND NIGHT THINGS the dominant thrust is one of diving, burrowing, disappearing into Night/ Death/Non-ness. And always there remains the mostly-unfulfilled need for "contact," The Liebestod Loved One accompanying her as she descends into this cyclic Country of the Dead waiting rebirth.

In practical, everyday terms what we're seeing here is Middle-Class housewife Lifshin discarding her Meat School (and every other "assumed") I.D. and allowing herself to go through a kind of Dark Night of Identity, trusting that on the other side of the darkness she will take on an identity of totally her own light. LEAVES AND NIGHT THINGS is a document of negation, suspension, disintegration, phase one in an extended process of affirmation, resumption, re-integration. How long does this "period" last, while in it what kinds of variations/facets does it manifest? 1970, moving into 1971.

NOTES

[1] "Office," in LEAVES AND NIGHT THINGS, no pagination.
[2] *Ibid.*, "The Right Techniques."
[3] "John B."
[4] "New England Sea Night of Snow Lips, Visions."
[5] The original has "sneared" instead of "sneered."
[6] "I should have been a pair of ragged claws/Scuttling across the floors of silent seas," 11. 73, 74.
[7] From "Potatoes."

CHAPTER III

In a sense Lifshin's 1971 volume BLACK APPLES[1] is merely a variation on LEAVES AND NIGHT THINGS, in another it represents a departure into new latitudes, a taking on of new weights, dimensions....

First of all BLACK APPLES comes to grips with Lifshin's "real" Jewish past, with grandfathers, fathers, uncles. She's re-ordered the past, given herself a psychic context, fabricated a continuum, a past:

> My father in his
> sister's dark house
> chanting like a
> Jew,

and her saying "Beryl, his/sleek Hebrew name,/I didn't even know/I knew it," unconsciousness knowledge, the Past having seeped into without her knowing it. And is there some sort of identification with her/her-father's mystical Jewish past, his (her) transcendental "communing" with the secret nature of things that she sees in him, but is unwilling to re-see in herself?

> In Vermont in
> rooms plain grey and
> wooden
> I remember his sitting
> those nights without
> a word and
> how he stood in the park,
> listened to chestnuts dropping.
> But not much else.[2]

The picture that emerges of her "origins," the psychograms of her childhood, ancestral "context," is of very closed, private people who—like her father immersed in the park-world of dropping chestnuts—guarded themselves, maintained their links to their past (and present) without any sharing. Like the grandmother who never gave either the Lithuanian city where she was born and grew up or herself,[3] or the grandfather who—again guarded—"confided his regrets mostly to the redmaple wind."[4]

What we have here is a familial nucleus of "presencers," mystic gnostic types who commune with the Presences in the world around them. And possibly Lifshin's own "presencing" derives from this early environmental conditioning that by its very fine-tuning acuteness, its awarenessing to the Invisible world under the surface of the everyday, even further separated the poet from her peer group's total *lack* of this kind of awarenessing. In one very revealing poem, "The Visit," haunted by the "presences" of Family, Lifshin says that although she can never really enter totally into the dynamics of the family mystique, at the same time she can never really escape from it either, but remains "borderline," neither part of one or the other world, an eternal outsider, participating in everything but never an integral part of anything:

> Later in the day we leave, put the heavy love at a distance
> These images can never be unified
> or undone.

Here, although we're often in a secret drowned underwater world, unlike its analogue in LEAVES AND NIGHT THINGS, the poet is seldom totally alone and there is very little sense of total abandon/The Drowned. The psychic landscape may slant toward water, skirt the water's edge (as in "Poem for the House Being Eaten by Water") but there are escape routes "out," other alternatives to self-immolation.

> The whole house
> slants to the lake
> water coming
> deep to one side
> up to your knees. . . .
> If you come over
> anytime, just
> don't leave
> by the
> back door

At times, Lifshin seems beyond the *need* for love (roots/ ties). The fear of drowning/immolation seems past and she's beginning to nibble on a sense of solitary independence that doesn't even want the moulding pressure of The Other:

> Love, you are like that
> distant water, pulling
>
> and twisting,
> you turn me
>
> apart from myself
> like some frightening road. . . .

which ends with a kind of "letting go," flowing with the currents into a quiet haven of humming existential Now:

> . . . let my
> hair float slow through
> this new color,
> let my eyes absorb
> all light
>
> from this turning
> that has brought us
> here, has carried us
> to where we are,
> we are,[5]

With a strong emphasis on the ARE. The "we" is deemphasized, the whole process of resistance to "influence" ("pulling and twisting") is consigned to irrelevance. The Now becomes all. Almost simultaneously with the recognition of mystic "awareness" in her family/tradition, Lifshin finds the same traits/dynamics in herself.

In fact the whole association-complex of The Drowning Woman here assumes a curious transmutation into water not as death but conductor into The Now. In "I'd Like to Live Here a While It's All," for example, Lifshin arrives at the mystic turning-point of Zen "zeroness" when she finds herself no longer needing love/the love "crutch," content to hover in a Now that is stripped of all content, a kind of surrender to a contemporary Cloud of (Mystical) "Unknowing":

> so open the house
> floats to the lake
> sun lights up the webs
> i'd wait for the
> leaves to grow close
> water make love to my
> thighs....
>   i could forget
> i ever wanted to be
> your lady, letting the
> rusty wind in, listening
> to nothing

Of course there is a lot of strong "sensorialness" in BLACK APPLES with its "lilac hills"[6] and the tastes of "lemons in the wind,"[7] and much of the volume is filled with the "blood glow"[8] of a sexuality that is especially poignant and cast into relief by a context of cold, rain, outside "interruption." There's even one poem—"Nice"—which is a sexual-graphic triumph with its juices and nails and raw stems and "licked flesh oil/waves lunging," but under all the celebration of flesh/The Now you can feel the infrastructure of "emptiness," the abiding contact between The Poet and the mystical Unknown/Unknowable.

The fleshed-out Now remains fragile, always in danger of turning into "un-reality,"[9] and there remains a constant threat of violence/Death:

> I am that
> girl let's say and you, if you
> are there might hear the
> bodies getting louder and
> louder, as tho
> something inside was
> near breaking
> tho right now everything
> is at the still
> edge of a scream.[10]

In BLACK APPLES, then, Lifshin has already left her Meat School mask behind, has begun to rediscover her mystic "past," begun to find in herself a Transcendental Communicator with "Things," close, very close to the humming mystic center where

Self vibrates in tune with the Cosmic, still somewhat hanging on to flesh/the moment/love, but already casting off into a sea-world that doesn't represent drowning as much as it does self-encounter so that the fear of leaving the bourgeoisie self is gone and the psychonaut has already—even within a limited radius—begun to voyage. The impressive thing is how soon the poet begins to beam in on the targets of her quest. The whole "self" is already there, aware, "moving." Now the question is—does the trajectory remain the same, is the line steady, or is this just one of a series of metamorphic selves/possibilities/"lives."

NOTES

[1] NEW BOOKS, The Crossing Press, Trumansburg, New York
[2] "Beryl," no pagination.
[3] "Never the City's Name."
[4] "Family."
[5] "Light From this Turning."
[6] "Light From this Turning."
[7] "Lemon Wind."
[8] "Mustache."
[9] "Lust Blowing Under the Door, Bright as Straw": ". . . those small/bones that changed her/small/bones to water/And not even/knowing/his name/until later/when the floor fell/the room/turned into a/painting/and the paint cracked."
[10] "Hear the Bodies Getting Louder."

CHAPTER IV

LADY LYN (Hey Lady Supplement No. 15, Morgan Press, 1971) is almost pure "existence," the working out of the existential theories/projections already formulated in BLACK APPLES. BLACK APPLES diagrams the concrete working-out of the scenarios in LADY LYN. LADY LYN takes the whole dynamics of "presencing," of feeling the invisible "hums" in the environment and carries them over into pure practice:

>   your lady
>   this torn
>   house   the
>   weeds   love we
>
>   could just
>   watch the
>   lake
>
>   in one corner
>
>   listen to
>   leaves to
>   what the
>
>   shutters say
>   nights[1]

The importance of "The Other" is diminished to the point of passive, almost invisible "witness." The "he"/lover is reduced almost to the point of being "implied," and the emphasis is shifted to the voicings of things—here leaves, shutters . . . the night. The poet has shifted, then, from any need to belong to affective reality and has been able to open all stops/barriers/screens between Self and the secret voices of the Out There.

Sometimes the mystic union (again a return to the image of the classic medieval Cloud of Unknowing) is complete. Contact made . . . and then "fulfilled":

> moving thru a
> thick blue
>
> go and that
>
> fog comes
> into me
>
> my one lover[2]

It's not that she's totally inside "the cloud," engulfed by the Presences, nor that the Presences are totally benign. In fact the nature of the "Out There"/fog/"divinity" remains epistomologically ambiguous. Like in "What's":

> Lying
> here in the dark I
> think of the possibilities.
> If you don't put the
> lights on suddenly
> we'll never see
> what's crawling near us.

We're not in the presence of any evil-less, benign, optimistic Hindu or New England Brahmin transcendentalism here, but a transcendentalism that distrusts the nature of the transcendent. Lifshin does effect a self-emptying, an empathizing . . . "contact." But with what?

> the trees a
> flaming
> orange
>
> I lie with my
> legs twisting
> yr back
>
> thinking
> this
>
> is me
>
> yellow flowers.
> the trees
> come after us[3]

The world turns paranoically negative, the Force of Evil isn't just "there," but actively "against"/"attacking." We're suddenly in the world of the Anti-Romantic, the agony of perceiving the destructive presence of "evil":

> please don't
> go the blue
> air's full of
> poisoned wings. . . .[4]

And at times with a Dantean equation between hell and cold, reality suddenly freezes over: "every//day's blue/monday, the/ birds are/made of ice."[5]

Simultaneous with this cosmic perception of evil, though, there's a whole other human side to the reality of LADY LYN. There's the old need for/lack of "love ("the/rain the way it/beats a/code to/get here,/to say oh/please love/hurry"), a poignant referencing to what seems to be a lost/aborted (?)/miscarried(?) child ("My baby gone/pasted to a/hill in Colorado . . ."),[6] a touching sense of distancing, alienation, solitude that culminates in a scenario of an imagined snowman lover:

> i should make
> myself a
> man of snow
>
> these holidays
> seem like
> someone else's[7]

So that Lifshin as "philosopher-mystic," at the same time that she's logically merging with the "life in 'thing'," (with all its menacing negativity) is simultaneously singing (as poet/'communicator') a fragmented song of essential aloneness/alienation.

It's difficult to find anywhere else in the contemporary scene this particular combination of advanced mysticism and "pop sentiment." Luckily Lifshin never shifts entirely into the mystic never-never land that ended up separating a D. A. Levy from "The Public," and at the same time she never falls into the personal "chattiness" that fails to ever "monumentalize" the very topical work of, say, a Wakoski. Lifshin somehow combines the accessible with the inaccessible, the essential condition of man with America A.D. 1970's-80's. She becomes the Voice of the Age, the Spokeswoman of the Zeitgeist, summing up in herself the whole trajectory of existential *angst* that sprouts from occidental philisophical-artistic soil at the beginning of the nineteenth century and perhaps finds its culmination in our American post-industrial decline and fall.

A poem like "After Hearing the News I Start Falling" begins and goes nowhere, hovers in its own corroding juices, secretes its own pain and baleful self-awareness, and sums up a whole *condition* of uneasiness, uncertainty, ambiguity, both personal and national:

> gray sand,
> a palm
>
> cold fingers I
> fold into
> myself
> like
> a brain
>
> the swollen river
> sinks in, roots
> that twist
> nowhere

It's irrelevant here whether the "news" is personal or "political;" what's important is the reaction of the Existential Self to any form of intrusion from the Out There. The core idea of Self versus Wounding Environment transcends the individual and this whole process of "folding" into itself "like a brain" neatly captures the whole business of alienation/"outsiderness."

The house here *is* "torn,"[8] the trees *do* come after her/them,[9] there *are* things out there "crawling near" them,[10] the poet *does* feel like "half of a geode . . . /wondering/where what/was whole/went,"[11] . . . the whole world here takes on a sinister, sentient cast. Lifshin fulfills the promise of her familial "mysticness," she does feel the menacing sub-surface Presences inside things. With LADY LYN she steps outside the ring of the "competition," becomes a "school" unto herself, leaves behind whatever could be construed as techniques or ideas that come out of her precedessors, whether Plath, Secton, or . . . LADY LYN is that kind of a pathfinding book, a step out into Self. Here we begin to feel outselves in the presence of a great original.

NOTES

[1] "Please Let Me Be," no pagination.
[2] "Blue."
[3] "Glimmer Glass Lake."
[4] "More Reasons Not To."
[5] "Every Day The. . . ."
[6] Both of these quoted from "Rain."
[7] "December."
[8] "Please Let Me Be."
[9] "Glimmer Glass Lake."
[10] "What's."
[11] "Pieces of You."

CHAPTER V

It's too simple to say that MOVING BY TOUCH[1] is the obverse side of LADY LYN, that the "presences" are still there but somehow they've become benign, although there is that element of reversal here in the title-poem:

> that afternoon an
> unreal amber
> light 4 o'clock   the
> quietness of
> oil   february   blue
> bowls full of
> oranges . . we were
> spreading honey, butter
> on new bread our
> skin nearly
> touching
> even the dark wood glowed[2]

In statistical terms MOVING BY TOUCH does represent a shifting toward benignity, although the same strains of thematic negativity continue on here too. Like in "Deserted House" with its echoes of the 1st child, the emptiness . . . not dissolved, not torn, but progressing toward The Vacant/Absent:

> Blue glass in
> the earth
> floor, the
> windows gone.
> Deserted
> house, my
> baby missing
> too. Paint
> pulls from the
> wood. In the

> wind apples
> roll thru the
> torn door.[3]

House, of course, is a personal, psychic symbol in the Lifshin canon, but tends to become here with its earth floor and windowlessness/paintlessness, something more, a new synapse established in the Lifshin nerve-network. She's not just basking in the Here and Now, but sending out exploratory "shoots" trying to encounter (create!) a personal past. In a sense the "floating" begins to end here; she moves from Perceptor out of context to Perceptor in a definite historical time-stream. The Indian enters in:

> in your room of
> sun and metal
>
> ghosts of indians
> the barns crumbling
>
> wormwood inside us
> only we didn't know
>
> saw only the ice
> cones dripping the
>
> sheets tangle smelling
> good you said
>
> as a woman had been there[4]

The "woman" may have been there, there may be a recrudesence of the personal, the "Meat," the psychic bed-tumbling rush into the Here and Now, but the new element here is the "ghosts" of Indians, thematically tied in to a stripping bare, back to bone, earth, The Essential.

The Psychic Explorer here begins a whole new "tack." She still doesn't penetrate, get inside, but MOVING BY TOUCH is an exercise in "awarenessing," stage one in getting inside/identifying:

> drove for days in
> the rose and blue
> light of the desert
> stoned on names

> ocotillo, coral bean
> by the sixth day the
> aloneness got us   there
> wasn't a face or voice
> not even near the
> hogans   nights   we slept
> in the car with the
> doors locked   locked
> in ourselves we were
> like skin peeled from a
> finger, shrivelling
> having nothing to do
> with any hand[5]

We move to a zero-point of new-departures here. The journey is one of the renunciation that precedes new beliefs/acceptances. The movement away from The Crowd/The Urban/The Modern takes Lifshin into the silence of the Indian past. She gets inside the "names of things": ocotillo, coral bean . . . and then the moment of "dissociation" takes place between the old accepted/acceptable self and this new unknown, the Indian Past: "we were/like skin peeled from a/finger, shrivelling/having nothing to do/with any hand."

In Lifshin is constant life-death cyclicity, she goes through a series of "emptyings-out" and "re-fillings" in this quest-pattern of trying to find a way to "presence"/"feel"/"relate" in an environment that she essentially finds hostile, not "her." And here, by tendrilling back to the Amerindian past she penetrates whole layers of accreted "civilization" (false-selves) and by touching the (primitive) Indian past she touches primitive layers of her own stratified Self.

Take the highly sexualized image out of "Snake Dance" (p. 30) ("i could/be doing that snake/dance knowing about/things that bite and/what happens later still/taking them into my mouth") and superimpose it on the really key-poem of the whole book, "Last night i . . .":

> last night i
> dreamed the
> girl who was
> strangled in
> boston came

> with a neck
> lace of roots
> that seemed
> to be growing
> or were they
> snakes circling
> her throat? . . .⁶

What you have is a death-rebirth motif in which the rebirth occurs within the specificity of Amerindian ritual. Lifshin is reasserting her (specifically) feminine (N.B. "neck" separated from "lace") self in the context of Amerindia . . . and as if to cinch this I.D., the poem goes on: "i'd rather/think they were hairs of/rebirth like/in the film where the boy/grows his own/grandmother/out of her/death. . . ."

Death and rebirth become "racial" here. Up till now Lifshin has hovered within the "force-field" of her European-Jewish past, unable to incarnate into any viable American present. Now out of a surrogate-sacrificial-victim, the Boston strangulation-case, she dreams of her own death and literal (root) rebirth in which she emerges as one of the snake-ritual reborn *like someone born out of the death of her own grandmother.* Call it circles, links, metamorphosis, death sliding into roots that are snakes that are rebirth hairs associated with grandmother hair associated with rebirth out of her own ancestral past. The penultimate image in the poem brings this whole complex together:

> . . . . .he
> waters earth
> in his bed
> until a tree
> grows with
> her in it. . . .

In other words, *whatever rebirths Lifshin as individual may experience, her collective familial past goes with her!*

Even the sexuality in MOVING BY TOUCH becomes more "nativistically" primitive:

> foraging
> living on trees

> on mushrooms   stars
> on seaweed
>
> i drew landscapes
> on your penis
>
> air roots   we
> twisted   sucked on
> the sun[7]

Not "Mad Girl" at all as the title implies, but Sane Girl undergoing identity *change,* coupling herself into the mushroom-star-(snake)–sun symbolism of the Amerindian collective consciousness.

She never loses her sense of personal collective past ("a water of all/we've forgotten/flows over/the bed . . .)[8] but there are moments of reversion back to "The Civilized" that—by contrast with the very real smack of Indian earth, sky, hogan, snake, sun—take on the shimmer of irreality:

> 21 feet high in
> philadelphia   the
> no poem deep
> quiet   the
> february snow
> peeling away   i'm
> sitting near glass
> pulled into sun   into
> this poem
>   somehow far
> off un
> real like those
> roofs down there. . . . .[9]

The game is "presencing," the thrust into a pantheistic encounter with the Divine Now, and now that she's established her "course" (trajectory) she seems to find an inherent conflict between this encounter and The Occident. Interesting touch, for example, in "Monet's Les Nympheas" (an attempt to follow an Occidental Pantheistic Master), the insertion of a Chinese girl in the meditative exercise:

> the long curved
> room   the walls

> starting to
> shimmer   breathe
>
> a chinese girl
> sitting on the stone
> bench next to me
>
> dazed   smiling
>
> the lilies moving
> into both of us[10]

What are the "candles in us/saved for/something/like this/ emergency" but a spiritual reserve to save her from spiritual death, a kind of spiritual "doubling" effect whereby she can coexist in contemporary America and at the same time spirit-voyage to the Oriental in the American Past, i.e. Amerindian spirituality. "We move/by touch/," she goes on to say in the candle-poem, "melt and/are our/own roof/burning/against/the dark/rain."[11] The Occidental Self is consumed (burning) in the midst of contemporary pressurings (the dark rain—cf. Dylan's *hard* rain) and the touch-movement is another way of saying reversion to earlier selves, personal familial-historical resources.

MOVING BY TOUCH is an exercise in instinct, the Poet finding in American geography/history spiritual analogues that respond to her own deepest needs. You wonder why she's such a hermit and what voices speak to her in her hermitage. The water lilies, perhaps, but even more so the Zen-Amerindian past, a similar but much deeper response that Monet even achieved to the "voices" hidden inside our surrounding "things."

In one very revealing poem the whole dynamics come totally clear. Down the coast to see horses leaping into the water, the poet asking "What is it they/smell that/they plunge in?," then plunging into the exact same "something":

> horses coming
> from the other
> side from
> inside
>
> until i'm
> buried in some
> thing they
> are and

>   sun pulls
>   my blood too[12]

The pursuit of this "something" divine hidden inside the world, the invisible divinity waiting to be intuitively "presenced," by 1972 has become the focal point of the Lifshinian quest. Anything else is secondary, and as we shall see the whole socio-political context of the Seventies serve, if anything, as merely distraction, the buzzing of a Reality that for cabbalistic Lifshin, remains un-real, irreal, irrelevant. Horse, sun, hogan, earth, this is the main-line of her own reality and her single-minded pursuit of this meditative merging with reality is what separates her so radically from her contemporaries.

NOTES

[1] Cotyledon Press, 1972.
[2] *Ibid.*, p. 6.
[3] *Ibid.*, p. 10.
[4] "Snow Fences, Wormwood," p. 11
[5] "Chihuhua Coahuila," p. 14.
[6] *Ibid.*, p. 19.
[7] "Mad Girl's Song," p. 18.
[8] "This is," p. 28.
[9] "To Poem Or, Today You're Like a Phone I Almost Don't Answer, p. 20.
[10] *Ibid.*, p. 25.
[11] Untitled, p. 31.
[12] Untitled, p. 13.

CHAPTER VI

THE MERCUROCHROME SUN POEMS (Charas Press, 1972) fills out the picture of Lifshin in the early nineteenth seventies. We see her here not just as a contextual Poet, Poet in the Parnassian Abstract, but Poet in Time, the U. S., a world of misunderstanding, "prejudice," Yahooland:

> all of us sitting on the
> steps of the capital
>
> with poems for spring   there
> are 12 cops saying we can't
>
> say anything dirty no "tits"
> or "fuck"   they'll pull the
>
> plug   i don't know what to
> read and pick a poem called
>
> DANGLING PRONOUN this is
> terrible one cop says
>
> have you got another copy
> for me to bring the boys
>
> Next thing, it's raining[1]

The poet as performer, exposing herself to the pragmatic scrutiny of the American world. There's another poem about taping in a studio: "something/for fall that won't offend anyone in kansas."[2]

The poet as "citizen" in the early seventies afraid of mailboxes and radios as the Horror comes slowly filtering in:

> one more dead
> from in the mailbox

> lying on the floor
> listening to
> fire   light thru the
> bottom shade
>
> listening for more
>
> hoping the unofficial
> report on the radio's
> not true somehow[3]

Here you suspect that even the "personal" poems with their apocalypic-destructive images are "shadows" of/echoes of/ricochettings off the socio-economic "outer-reality." Like the hobo whose picture she takes:

> we took his
> picture   what he
> was drinking
> twisted the light,
> in the photograph
> it looked like blood[4]

Or the "something" coming through the woods in "The Dream of Holes," the final image where the poet comes looking for wild lilac and finds:

> .... the place was
> a hole I
> didn't
> understand
> the knives
> bloody seed
> or the girl
> crying who
> was me

It's not the thrust here as the very personal female-metamorphosed poems of the earlier volumes. It's not Lyn going through a series of death and resurrection rituals, but 1). An uncyclic resurrectionless levelling, 2). A destruction not of surrogate selves, but of entire landscapes:

> the 2nd night it's
> harder to sleep
>
> black horses against
> a blood sky. . . .
>
> If we were
> in a real
> war in this
> field
>
> would all this
> be luxury
> Is it now[5]

What are we to make of the military imagery of "these relics/torn buckles/coins, a/razor . . . the mangled bodies?"[6] There's some hint that we're in a museum-world of American slavery ("clay dropped/in flight in this/field of/chickery"), but then the stench of the very-contemporary military seems to come through:

> after the
> garrisons,
> penetration at the
> points where
> least expected
>
> Left clots of
> rusting shovels
> bones. . . .[7]

Isn't, for example, the poem that is ostensibly about burning poems really a recreation of the napalmed landscape of Vietnam?

> . . . . a
>
> whole orchard
> burning all night
> and into summer[8]

No question, the poet *wants* escape, the usual "distance," the glorying in the real-presences of divine-reality . . . but sociopolitical reality *intrudes* and the poet is drawn out of the bluebird almost dreamlike fin-de-siecle landscape of a Materlink or Baudelaire into the reality of her world (even peripherally) at war: "inside the/relics yellow//a letter is full of wounds//an old code//punishment for/desertion//1000 lashes."⁹

Simultaneous with this "intrusion" of "The Real," Lifshin "breaks out" into The Ideal again. An "ideal" (again) derived from Amerindian sources:

      a high mountain
    on a
      clay green
        island the
    plain thick
      with cattle
        deer
    roses and lindenberry

the spirit crosses the water

    on a tree that
    grows and
  grows
        only the
    good get
    anywhere.

This is the "Shawnee Idea of Heaven," Part I. The abode of the good. And the sinful: "wander/in a cold grey country/alone forever."[10]

National guilt becomes personal. The poet becomes "scapegoat" in a way, expiatory victim/Messiah taking on the sins of the world . . . the sacrificial lamb. Only the punishment instead of being crucifixion here becomes aloneness forever in a cold grey country—a beautifully oblique way of feeding back into the USA of the Viet Nam years.

You want The Poet to stay isolated, to have her "poems paper/moving like/leaves over/new snow my/own snow."[11] And even inside this envelope of national guilt, within the syntactical context of wounds, war, burning, isolation . . . "greyness," Lifshin the Transcendentalist transcends:

    trillium   starflower   stars
    rosewood   in the gallery
    roses   rose apple. . . .

> We woke up today
> and the leaves were greener
> than any i've lived near
>
> even poems, i didn't know
> they would be given
> if i was this happy[12]

Only even dreaming she can't escape the mercurochrome in the title:

> when the air's
> full of rain
> that's when I
> run into you in
> the parking lot
> of macy's   or
> maybe it's
> the desert   a
> mercurochrome
> sun, i can't tell
> if i'm smiling
> or in pain
> because i keep
> forgetting
> what i
>   Then i
> wake up shaking[13]

She's not running into a SOMEONE. The title isn't "Running into Someone UNDER a Mercurochrome Sun," but "Running Into Then Losing the Mercurochrome Sun." The encounter is with the medicinal, "treated," wounded sun, and in the encounter she loses her own sense of diagnosis/awareness . . . it's only when she wakes up that she returns into herself and then she knows the encounter has been with a depersonalizing sense of "war."

THE MERCUROCHROME SUN POEMS are a kind of climax in Lifshin's life, an unbearable peak of pain/"involvement." You can only expect that the next book in the chronology of the canon, will be a total rejection of this futile suffering for suffering's sake, a spirit-trip by water to the cattle-thick island of Shawnee Heaven as if she's saying "The proper business of *this* poet anyhow, is the pursuit of the Sacred, not a negative participation in the Profane."

NOTES

[1] "Poetry Reading," no pagination.
[2] "Tape," n.p.
[3] "July Friday," n.p.
[4] "White Lilac in the Rubble Half a Chair," n.p.
[5] Untitled, "the 2nd night . . . ," n.p.
[6] Untitled, p. 36.
[7] Untitled, n.p.
[8] "Burning Poems," n.p.
[9] Untitled, p. 40. Lifshin's own comment on this line of approach: "The relics are based on wandering around the Saratoga Battlefield . . . I wrote it at Yaddo and tho I don't know if I was consciously thinking of Viet Nam—it certainly does now that you mention it echo that—how could it not. They were written in May or so of 1970 around the Kent State riot times . . ." (Letter, April 25, 1981).
[10] *Ibid.*, p. 26.
[11] "On a Morning Like This," n.p.
[12] "Gifts," n.p.
[13] "Running Into Then Losing the Merchrochrome Sun," n.p.

CHAPTER VII

MUSEUM (1973)[1] is precisely that, a total and violent shift out of "real" into "mythical" Amerindian time. It's as if the poet has said "Enough of the present, let me shift peacefully back into a past—that I hope to make mine...."

MUSEUM begins with ceremonies of The Dead:

>   the face of the
>   dead
>   painted on the
>   coffin
>   they brought what he'd
>   need
>   grain   a boat
>   a woman....[2]

She examines their artifacts . . . and interestingly the "their" takes in the totality of Amerindia with little distinction as to tribe, location, difference. The vision is whole, the mind-projection back is not to a single place of identity but to a whole lost world-view:

>   maya cache
>   figure of a
>   woman
>   no breasts but her
>   cunt like a
>   huge valley
>   Flint obsidian jade
>   shell
>   shaped into scorpion and
>   centipede
>   priest's teeth
>   inlaid with
>   jade
>   in an orange lidded

> pottery jar
> its meaning
> largely unknown[3]

Lifshin dwells on Indian sexuality here, something more open/real/"genuine" than herself trapped in The Occident. She's fascinated with the Indian sense of "decoration," extravagant surface. And above all she's blocked, frustrated by the wall of The Unknown that surrounds this impenetrable dead past.

The antiquity of lost Amerindia teases at her:

> 2 small babies
> held in
> dryness
> they found these mummies in a
> limestone cave
> born in
> new mexico around the
> time of
> beowulf[4]

She reaches out to understand their ritual, the "3 pieces of pottery as a burial/offering," dwells again on decorative color/size: "the blue/clay jars/bigger than the baby."[5]

And then in Poem 4 she reveals the Why behind all the persistence of interest in ritual. It's not just the number of items buried with a body in a particular configuration. The mechanical gives way to purpose. The newborn infant in Poem 4 was buried beneath the floor of the mother's house

> with the hope that the
> spirit might be
> reborn,
>
> come back to her
> in the flesh again[6]

In this return to the resurrection theme, Lifshin has found a whole culture she can share her needs with. She's penetrated through Mystery (and a sense of "separateness"/The Alien) into shared need, moved out of the resurrectionless materialism of the contemporary to another layer of spiritualist American past— a rejection of the present and recognition of her own spiritual antiquity.

She's fascinated by Ideals overcoming the ordinary sense of self-survival, the Abstract overcoming The "Human." "Victims" were buried with chiefs, an idea she keeps coming back to, "living sacrifices," and she wonders "were they/drugged/did they/lie there/waiting/for the reed mat for earth/to fall upon them?"[7]

In one particularly lapidary, image-encrusted poem she shifts suddenly down out of the southwest to Panama and focuses in on "twenty-three men and woman/buried/alive," and abruptly juxtaposes this "sacrifice" against the oriental richness of the gravefinds:

> the
> gold is practically pure
> crocodile with a huge
> emerald in his
> back,[8]

so that the magnitude of the "sacrifice" is enclosed within a context that raises it up from the rites of "savages" to the ceremonies of king.

She gets involved with and practically unravels the mystery of Amerindian origins. "No one knows where/they/came from" she says, *but* "old cloth shows birds animals and/sea beasts,"[9] and she re-stresses the sea-motifs in Amerindian art and artifacts:

> all sea creatures
> especially
> the octopus
> flourished in their
> art[10]

You can't help but wonder if these surrogate-projections into the mystery-origins of the Amerindians isn't a kind of re-living of her own mystery-origin past. She glories in the richness of Amerindian artifacts, their sea-journey link to other worlds, their sense of ordered, ritualistic pomp, decorativeness at the service of The Sacred. In fact there's a congruity between Lifshin and the Amerindian sense of sacredness that pacts them together against the whole occidental sense of The Sacred that Lifshin has been rebelling against all her life without really being able to put a name to it. Here god is immediate, raw, experiential, not a question of conservative, "inside" worship, but a confrontation out in the open that turns The Savage, really, into the

Totally Permeable, Transcendentalism as a way of everydayness:

>   never threatened by
>   invasion
>   they made no
>   walls
>   wanting to let the
>   sun in
>   the men rode
>   into trees
>   to hunt. . . .
>   they worshipped in caves in
>   orange groves
>   on mountain tops. . . .[11]

Isn't she reduplicating her familial sense of divine immediacy that in turn itself reduplicates the ancient middle east? Isn't she finding the historically valid link between Lifshin, the exile, ashamed (almost) to admit the "energy" that she feels swirling in reality around her, and the Amerindian past that lived in existential, daily contact with this same "energy?"

How revealing the juxtaposition in Poem 8 of the ritual burial ground in Panama where the chief was buried alive with his wives and helpers and the present day reality of a coffee plantation that was built on *top* of the cemetery, the enemy (commerce) thereby obliterating the essential religious past:

>   dug up in 1940   8
>   feet under a
>   coffee plantation. . . .

Finally at the end of MUSEUM Lifshin tires of its "mu= seumness." Indians as scholarly-guessing aren't enough:

>   . . . . i wanted
>   more   the hands
>   fingers that
>   twisted this
>
>   ring of
>   split yucca
>
>   what the
>   blood dreamed

> flesh rubbing the
>   clay to a
> black glow[12]

The kindship she feels moves from theoretical to experiential, she time-travels back into the empty ruined world of Amerindia and takes on its guise/experience/worldview. She never really leaves Amerinda from now on; in fact even when she time-travels into The Colonial Whiteworld now, she travels mostly inside the skins of Indians. She's found a permanent historical analogue for her "outsiderness," a world that encompassed as normal a complex ritualism for death, life, daily-living, permanetly and continuously in contact with Presences that are slight variants of the Presences that the poet already brings with her to her "projections." She *does* dream what the blood dreamed. It would have been interesting if she could have gone *further* into this analogue Indian world, travelled, lived, *become* . . . but her radical empathy essentially does what anthropology often can't—wears the skin and sees through the eyes of the subjects who with her never become "objectified" but merely kindred mystics.

Civilization, finally, becomes *the* soul-killer—and even those *Indians* who survived into whiteman-times were corrupted.

In fact she has one poem that is in a sense a History of the Decline and Fall of All Civilization, the Cochise beginning semi-savage ("lived on wild plants/pemmican and/dried roots"), with almost no tools ("just these/grinding tools for/vegetables/choppers of/quartzite"), with the simplest almost touching rites for the dead ("they offered the/dead/bluebird feathers"), slowly becoming more sophisticated, learning metallurgy ("flint/speaks a/copper dagger") finally adopting the arms of The West ("firearms") along with occidental "games,"at this point the *real* savage emerging, now no longer enclosed in the sacred in which blood-/blood-sacrifice is subordinated to higher ends, but in a world of cruel secularization:

> finally an apache
> poker case
>   the cards
> made of
> human skin.[13]

Call MUSEUM Time-Voyage I into the American past.

Back to the sacred, prehistoric mainly unaccessible world of an Amerindian msytique with which she finds all sorts of links and sympathies.

1973, she refuses to (still) come back to The Present, stays in her poetry-time machine and begins to voyage *toward* the Present wearing an aura of aboriginal sacred savagry around her.

Next stop THE OLD HOUSE ON THE CROTON.

NOTES

[1] Published by Conspiracy Press in Albany, New York, text accompanied by surrealistic collages by Eric Von Schmidt.

[2] First poem, unnumbered. For the rest of the book I'll just refer to poem number.

[3] 2.

[4] Poem 3.

[5] *Ibid.*

[6] Poem 4.

[7] Poem 5.

[8] Poem 8.

[9] Poem 9.

[10] Poem 6. I found Lifshin's perceptions of the sea-links of the Indians particularly acute because of my own researches into Amerindian origins. See GODS OF THE CATACLYSM, Harper's Magazine Press, 1976.

[11] Poem 6.

[12] Poem 11.

[13] Poem 7.

CHAPTER VIII[1]

THE OLD HOUSE ON THE CROTON[2] is another time-poetry trip, this time back to colonial upstate New York (Croton-on-the-Hudson)—the Van Cortland House.

It begins with pedestrian accounting-like exactness, biodata style:

> one son
> traded beaver down the hudson
> became mayor
> had 14 children
>
> for the land from here to
> peekskill paid the
> kitchawanac 50
> lbs of powder 8
> guns coats. . . ,[3]

but by the end of the exactness has become existential and she's taken on the coloration of the house and times, projected herself back out through the eyes of the house's inhabitants, resurrected them and then taken possession of them, reliving their world as they originally lived it. Even down to specific names/people. Like Cornelia, born in a bed with cracks in it that are still there:

> 21 years
> later pulling the
> curtains around them both
>
> that first night
>
> lay there next
> morning maybe
> touching her thighs
> doves in the black locust

> stared in this mirror
> for the difference
> in her eyes[4]

One theme that runs throughout the whole book that has tangential points with MUSEUM is the feeling for The Natural. We're not in Amerindian Sacred Time, but the Sacred Time of— at least—the Pre-Industrial when the whole relation between even the whiteman and the sensorial was more immediate, raw, "savage":

> smell of bread
>
> lemons oranges limes the
>
> sweet wood, roots burning. . .
>
> she hangs dried beans
> apples, herbs
>
> Deer come to the window.[5]

An interesting dichotomy is set up between The Male and The Female. The Female, yes, is in contact with The Senses, but the Men—and the war of men—are abstract, more *self*-involved than involved with the flow of reality around them. Letters are "carved on the fireplace/by hessian soldiers," (Poem 25) "guerillas from both sides" loot the house (Poem 19), at another point the "British burst in," (Poem 20) . . . we have the Male War Sphere enclosing and in a sense dominating the Female Domestic Sphere where the real existential interchange takes place. Lifshin really has passed through two "escape-loops" here in order to get back to her own existential present, back through time and then once in that "other" time, through the loop of The Female into an analagous colonial world that practically replicates her own. Hints of death/the grave again, the poem on the root-cellar a small trip into the grave where the non-conscious communings take place:

> root cellar
>
> built into the slope of earth
>
> moist cool even in august
>
> the children in the orchard
>
> a young woman   her hands
> smelling of rosemary

> slips out of a cotton shift
>
> earth holding her like water[6]

In one other poem this tomb-analogy turns totally explicit. She projects-out, smells ("room smelling of clay and/candles"), touches ("this black wax/caked on her fingers") and then completes the identification:

> no windows
>
> Did it seem like a
> tomb to her too[7]

THE OLD HOUSE ON THE CROTON has a funereal pall over it. The woman's world, which here is curiously enclosed in and dominated by The Male, for all its sensory heightening, its journeying into the olfactory-tactile Now, remains confined, controlled . . . narrow . . . tomblike. The Amerindian world, even as sexual, vaginal-centered female, has meant openness for her, a frank dialogue with Nature; here Nature comes filtered through War, and the female-world is relegated to partial perception, the servicing of the Other (Male) Mystique. The men "talked of war/ and money smoked/played chess,"[8] whereas the women dream of a kind of freedom that's expressed in love-fantasizing about a "journeyman weaver," until they face up to the reality of their "confinement" (again tomb/prison):

> . . . . the
> youngest daughter
>
> touching the beams over her
> head sighing
> will stay here with her
> parents till they die
>
> knows this
> climbs up shivering
> pulls the blue linen
> curtain of the bed
> as tight as she can around her[9]

Nowhere is this sense of Woman Confined more pointedly

expressed than in Poem 17 where a woman "cold in november" is kind of hidden away on the second floor of the house, receiving "the news" (of the American Revolution?),

> ...... closing this
> book wrapping wool
> tighter across her nipples[10]

Being enclosed, entombed, confined in place, in clothes themselves, hearing the "news" coming violently from an Out There of Male Consciousness that searingly violates her feminine sharpened-awareness, this is the picture of The Colonial Woman that emerges in Lifshin . . . and the Other World of "The Primitive" where Lifshin rightly feels that Woman is glorified instead fo confined, where does that stand in relation to this oh-so-white world?

The Indians are long-vanished/vanquished, shadowy figures out of Nevermore:

> .... Black
> sky ghosts
>
> of indians
>
> thru the branches[11]

And the Blacks—which never arrive at the front-stage-center importance of Indians in the poet's mind—still move mutely in the background, "slaves bringing in wood/from the smoke house/ just before the//new law. . . ."[12]

Stylistically, in THE OLD HOUSE ON THE CROTON, Lifshin reaches a new high-water mark of condensation/concision/ pointillistic "vibratoriness." Small hints are laid on the page and you have to step back and "distance" in order to really see them. Silk hangs on a branch to dry (Poem 4), you're touched by "grass//lilac, bees" (Poem 5), you walk under apple and pear trees, notice the ominous richness of a "darkstone purple floor" (Poem 6), watch the "snow pile against the/leaded pane" (Poem 7), touch the beams over your head (Poem 8) . . . it's a strangely "immediate," tactile journey, this book, a virtuoso performance of getting inside the skin of the Long Dead, reliving the historical. Lifshin as Beat Performer in the Bukowski tradition, is replaced by a poetic historian whose word-palate has all the desire to capture the moment of a Monet or Seurat. At the same time, though, you know she can't rest *here,* that she hasn't found herself in the sensory isolation of these women shunted aside and bottled up in a world of male violence. THE OLD HOUSE ON THE CROTON is one of many tentative excursions into otherlives, other-incarnations, but certainly not an affirmation of any positive identification with this particular time-layer or epistomological style. One thing she does seem to come away with, however, is the magic sense of "untreated" pre-industrial space, no industrial substratum of "noise"/"interference" between Viewer and Viewed. The roses are more roses, the moon on a box of knives (Poem 24) more moon, the "light on the chinese carpet" (Poem 25) much more evocative in this clear space than in any analagous excursion into the very contemporary. In a sense THE OLD HOUSE ON THE CROTON is another arrow pointing toward another necessary, positive direction—into a Now isolated from the buzz of the industrial. We get a clear picture of The Ideal for Lifshin and see why—as she once told me—so many poems were written at writer-artist "colonies." Substracting all the negatives of the colonial, one thing that Lifshin would have gloried in would have been the clarity of unaltered light and sound.

In 1974 another time-travel book came out that fits nicely into THE OLD HOUSE ON THE CROTON technique-scheme—WALKING THROUGH AUDLEY END MANSION LATER AFTERNOON AND DRIFTING INTO CERTAIN FACES.[13]

It's a quiet-toned, muted little book centering on Death and Time:

>how long will a thumb
>print
>stay on silver...
>
>How long will hair stay hair[14]

The fact that she's in England hardly matters because although you might expect the sense of EXILE to end with the English at "home," it doesn't, and the whole book is *still* filled with a feeling of "displacement," "foreignness":

>were the pale english days
>made brighter with these
>paintings of venice...

> Did it help to open
> the stuffed bird with
> green feathers brought
> by a viscount from
> Austria...[15]

The message is that a sense of belonging/place can't be concocted no matter how much you try; it must proceed (anticipating the message of the whole body of Indian and Eskimo poems) from a sense of tribalness. Unity, belonging, feeling at home in the world is a portable entity and doesn't really reside in place so much as in the individual woven within a world of "tribalness." Which is totally lacking here where the attempt to create an artificial world-outside-the-world manages to merely concoct the horror of ISOLATION:

> Stuffed birds in a
> cage   in a
>
> glass case pistols
> carved bones
>
> ivory face pasted in a
> boxgold writing
> in the shadow....
>
> ...her bedroom...a
> trip someplace else
>
> her world of peacocks
> snakes and jade trees....
>
> she must have felt like
> something under glass
> too...[16]

The Male here is typically Anglo-Saxon "mental," detached, distanced, cold, the Female forced into a chill, bitter isolation:

> woman twisting in
> chill sheets...
>
> Who is rubbing her
> hands near the fire

> now letting what
> they're full of
>
> rise thru the
> chimney into the fog[17]

    In a sense by being English/in England the AUDLEY END poems represent the quintessence of all the various isolations that Lifshin is against: Male isolated from Female, Individual isolated from the Land/Country, Mind isolated from Body. The English Mystique that we see transplanted to the American old-house poems represents a radical cutting-off of the individual from existential-experiential ROOTS. Here she traces the Beast to its lair. Colonial American "splitting"/"isolation" is merely an extention (watered-down) of this basic Anglo-Saxon trait.

NOTES

[1] Between MUSEUM and THE OLD HOUSE ON THE CROTON appeared a second edition of BLACK APPLES, but as Malone notes in his bibliography (WORMWOOD REVIEW, Number 59): "Expanded text ... adding 13 poems from WHY IS THE HOUSE DISSOLVING and LEAVES AND NIGHT THINGS" which we've already dealt with in their appropriate time-strata.
[2] Shameless Hussy Press, 1973.
[3] No pagination, Poem 2.
[4] Poem 26.
[5] Poem 14.
[6] Poem 12.
[7] Poem 15.
[8] Poem 9.
[9] Poem 8.
[10] Poem 17. The book referred to is the bible.
[11] Poem 23.
[12] Poem 23.
[13] Mag Press, Long Beach.

[14] *Ibid.*, p. 3.
[15] *Ibid.*, p. 5.
[16] *Ibid.*, pp. 11-12.
[17] *Ibid.*, p. 7.

CHAPTER IX

Although 40 DAYS APPLE NIGHTS was *published* in 1974, it really belongs to an earlier time-frame. A little help from Malone's bibliography here:

1. "1974; although copyright page reads 1972,"

2. "The originally announced title was I'D BE JEANNE MOREAU."[1]

So we're really back in the world of LADY LYN, MOVING BY TOUCH, THE MERCUROCHROME SUN POEMS, Lifshin in time, preplateau, pre-Buddha, pre-nirvanic Zen.

Perhaps the most revealing poem in the volume is "I'd be Jeanne Moreau and," which, while expressing a desire for escape from "time," also contains one of the old familiar drowning and resurrection images.

She wants to "never have to/make choices//living in the house with you"—suspension *and* "engagement"—but at the same time:

> . . . . . i would be
> going down for
>
> gold   drive off
> the bridge   It's
> all for you you
> know so look
> stunned   look
>
> down into these
> dark waves   moan
>
> so i can come back   seaweed
> in my hair   shells
> for a hundred
> jules and jim
> each one screaming me, me.[2]

Here as in all her pre-plateau poems, Lifshin vascillates between intense Now-perception and a distracting, negative entanglement with "the social"/sexual/shared:

> jasmine tea,
> iced apples
>
> hair fell across
> my face drifting
> upstairs
> in a sweet
> smoke, cherry
> burning, this
> paper smells
> of those
> fires. i
> want to too.[3]

Sometimes she's almost back to Bukowski-Lifshin again, totally out in the open, caught in the man-trap, fighting for a minimum space of personal territory:

> Listen, it's been
> enough, your
> whiskey lips
> don't move my
> snow like before,
> whatever it was
> it's used up,
> we just get low. . .[4]

Indians, when they do appear, aren't even mythic, museum-models, but something bookish/structuralistically analyzable: "rum and a strange iroquois/book from 1900." This strange Iroquois book describes the Iroquois practice ("only the suspicious") of burying "what precious things//they had in holes/or secret places," and suddenly in mid-poem Lifshin shifts from this structuralist distancing about suspicious Indians hiding their treasures to herself and her Man again: ". . . baby/when you looked //inside my red bag/poems, did//you think you'd/be in there"[5] which folded out seems to read: I AM LIKE THE SUSPICIOUS IROQUOIS WHO BURIED THEIR THINGS IN SECRET PLACES, MY SECRET PLACE IS MY BAG OF POEMS, ONLY

DON'T THINK YOU'LL BE THERE. Poem-territory, even in the midst of "sharing it," letting it be invaded, still is being set off as private/interior/secret. Poem-territory is her quiet interior place and any sharing at best is done begrudgingly.

There are even implicit dissertations On the Art of Poetry here, contrasts between ideal and disastrous psychological contexts in which the poet works optimally or minimally. Poems ideally become "ghost flowers" that

> ..... need
> decay too
> the rot of
> dark places.[6]

The poet ideally shouldn't compartmentalize, divide time into active-passive, social-isolated, but that's what (in this time-zone) she's had to do, a realization that comes to her with the grace of a Debussy arpeggio in a poem called "The First Week":

> i've been living in a house
> with paper partitions
> like in japan   keeping
> everyone separate
>
> but i didn't know that
> when i started this poem

So much self-probing, so many small operational-revelations here. You can see why she got to where she was going—the need for her life-fabric to be of all one piece, not patches, improvisations, all sorts of pullings, tensions, tears.

There's one deliciously ambiguous poem about what she doesn't want her poetry to be that, once-unravelled, tells it all:

> no i don't want the
>
> poems to be jars
> of dead children
> bees   safe ways of
> seeing something
> caught and
> over   the risk
> just on paper

> But worse that
> this possibility
> of ending up in
> that jar   keep
> you from me[7]

The key here being "safe ways of/seeing something/caught and/over," a whole SCHOOL of the "safe-poetry" that up to 40 DAYS, APPLE NIGHTS she'd avoided, the Wordsworthian-Sexton stance of using poetry as something definitely recollected in tranquility, not made (progressively) on the spot, in the middle of the action. Which is variant-repeated in "the risk/just on paper"—the reaction against separating The Life and the Art. MEN are the constant threat here in all these poems, during this whole *period* and it's not accident that here the jar (echo—bell-jar) image comes in twice: jars of "dead children/bees" and life itself as jar, "this possiblity/of ending up in that jar." The dead children is an image that recurs, but what about "bees"? Could the dead-hive, dead-children jar all revolve around Lifshin as trapped suburban housewife? What did she say to me about her married life in December of 1980?

> . . . he was insanely jealous. If I went out and say a man talked to me he'd get furious. So the first time I ever went anywhere, I got a fellowship to go to Boulder to a writer's conference, and he knew that I really cared about writing . . . and as soon as I got out there he said you can't stay there, you've gotta come back. . . .

Or (again talking about her husband, explaining the why of the early "meat-school-slant" in her poetry):

> . . . in my life, my real life, my life was so subdued and so . . . iolated and so . . . what's the word? I was living almost like a nun, really, my life was so secluded . . . protected. . . .[8]

Certainly throughout 40 DAYS, APPLE NIGHTS there's a straight-down-the-line dichtomy between The Creative/Freedom/Personal/Soft and The Controlled/Restriction/"Social" (read "Men")/Hard. Take a poem like "Fear" and its inherent panic at the presence of The Male:

> sitting here
> trying to remember
> exactly   he could
> have killed both
> of us   or am i
> imagining   he said
> don't use any of this
> (that strawberry
> dance in the bar)
> i was just glad to
> get away/hear some
> thing now   is that
> him knocking   i don't
> move   the papers
> blow like leaves
> a blue (his?) car
> roof gleaming
> like a knife

Especially powerful here the contrast between her isolation in the softness of her interiorness and the intrusion of The Male, the car, the knife (association). Or "Guitar Wood Leaves" with its image of Daphne turning into a tree, again the leaf-image ("my belly feels like leaves") and The Male coming in, returning to the wood-image (the poet herself as wood/tree):

> i wanted somebody with
> hands like his but
> i'm shaking   am
> just about to write
> this down when he
> walks in with
> the huge gibson
>
> for him all wood is
> something to play.

Of course what you feel above all else is the INSENSITIVITY. There's no blanket rejection/hatred on the poet's part. She stays permeable and receptive, even though (conditioned) somewhat cycnical. She exists in her own space which is systematically invaded by a (male) presence that doesn't comprehend, respond, adapt itself in any way to her. There really isn't any choice; it's either isolation *or* conforming totally to the form of The (masculine) Other.

On the one hand the poet wants "contact," on the other contact usually comes out defining itself as a kind of bondage. Take the poem "Thursday." Lifshin's alone in the house and begins to spin out a meditation:

> i
>
> start to read the
> eskimo poems but
>
> the light draws
> flying things. . . .

Here even light and its contact with life becomes a negative. What she'd *really* like is *total* isolation, a *total* participation in the phantasmagoric life of the poems. Then comes Degree One distraction ("flying things") followed by the return of The Male and an image that simultaneously suggests hanging and lasooing, victim and victimizer, prey and hunter:

> When you
>
> walk by under
> the window
>
> my hair turns
> into a rope.

In "Tuesday" again she flirts with empathetic, all-form-assuming passivity. Beginning in a blue universe mood ("Blue spruce a/slate blue sky//the blue car fear's gone") the omnipresent HE is singing "If Your Woman's Like a River," and the poet falls under the spell of passivity, not seeing herself as drowned and resurrecting, but totally self-formless, taking on the imposed form of The Male:

> you play 'if your
> woman's like
>
> a river.'
> i could
>
> be that water.

In a sense this flirtation with formlessness is the ultimate self-negation, a last ditch attempt for Lifshin "Le Poet Maudit," to simply disappear into a societally invisible, faceless woman-role. Self-destruction, up to now, was always filled with the potential of resumption of activity in other FORMS: HERE IT PLAYS WITH THE DYNAMICS OF BLEACHED NOTHING-NESS. Of if not quite bleached, then—at times—BLUE:

> Thinking of what a
>
> woman could be
>
> blue bed, the
> bluest blues
>
> There's so little
> not to share.[9]

"There's so little not to share," the feeling of being crowded, infringed on, invaded. What a woman *could be* is total passivity, but only within a context of depressed Blue Alert.

The whole book here is a study in the state of waiting, suspension, attached-detachment, all more or less summed up in "Drifting the":

> things i have and
> don't have
> come from this
> moving between
> people like leaves like
> smoke[10]

Again the passivity of leaves/smoke . . . followed by an image of herself as suspended milkweed puffs which in turn suggests hair and the miracle of how anything can stay so suspended (read "detached") in spite of the force of people-gravity/other-"wills"-gravity pulling it down. There's almost a definace here. "In spite of all the pressures I haven't 'collapsed,' 'conformed,' have toyed with the idea, but never given in":

> . . . . . I've been
> waiting the way
> milkweed i

Lyn Lifshin: A Critical Study

>brought inside 2
>years ago stays
>suspended   hair in the
>wind it seems to
>float   even its
>black seeds don't
>pull it down
>tho you don't under
>stand how any
>thing could stay
>that way
>so long

All in all, 40 DAYS, APPLE NIGHTS, by being out of step/phase/chronology, and reintroducing pre-plateau Lifshin into the rarefied, controlled Tibetan-cold world of The Plateau, vividly contrasts where she's come from with where she's going *to.* We've already seen her cast off from the present and time-travel back into alternative pasts. We've seen her sharpen her perceptions down to a final needle-point, turn from poster-paints to the most delicate pastels, withdraw from the madding crowd into the silence of isolated Self; and here we're reminded of all the pressures she's been fleeing *from,* the desire to "fit in" to the human love-community, the need for "the normal," accompanied always by the cankers of betrayal and control.

Poetry for her isn't a simple act of "painting," but a whole course of ascetic isolation, a monatic stripping away of Self from the social to the solitary, the shared to the searing vision of Self soaked in the essential Real.

By 1974-75 Lifshin had already solidified into her essential identity as existential explorer of the fine-tuned, ineffable, hieroglyphic, and her next volume, OLD HOUSE POEMS, represents this identity horizontally and vertically expanded, not so much a further exploration as a reiterative *affirmation!*

I should also make some mention here of another 1974 volume, POEMS, published by Konglomerati in Gulfport, Florida, a very revealing little set of poems still all about the membranously delicate problem of love-communication; and most revealing of all is the poem where (again) she relates her father's "distancing," self-involvement, interiorness, with her own problems of loving because loving, after all, is the most finely tuned manifestation of human communication:

>.............. We
> never talked and
> last week i met
> someone i wanted,
> i couldn't let
> him know.
> Now i dream i
> write him and the
> letters come back
> stamped rejected...[11]

The longing, the love-/-communication gap begins early, and in a sense is never "righted," the poetry itself becoming a surrogate means of breaking the solitude, filling it with at least imagined "bridges"/"ties":

> always imagining
> how something could
> be: i've seen things
> i might not have
>
> why else write
> about all the lovers
>
> and twist even this
> into a love
> poem for one of the
> men i didn't have[12]

POEMS also contains one of Lifshin's most "difficult," at the same time best poems about "alienation," really the same theme as in the father-poem, the very specific alienation of the unloved:

> mornings without
> a radio the
> wind full of
> clover. By
> noon tho
> who knows

> or when they
> unglue their
> smiles masks
> dissolve   they
> float over our
> houses sweat
> glittering
> on their foreheads
> The beads break
> first the bombs
> are small and
> some of us
> grab on to a
> pant leg
> When moons are
> they to make
> wolves of
> so many.[13]

The moons here are, presumably, The Suave Males, the were-wolves are The Seduced Women. She begins alone, "They" (the men) begin their generic "attack" the victims (like her) are transformed.

It's interesting to relate this poem to the father-poem above because it's almost as if they were two phases to the same psychological development, first rejection (The Father) and the creation of an Idealized Father, *then* the idealization feeding back from the reality of other men in a sinister domination/transformation of The Poet into controlled "slave."

Very similar in tone and theme to 40 DAYS, APPLE NIGHTS, POEMS represents one last small indulging in the sensitivities and confusions of Love before Lifshin begins to time-travel. It's one last look at Self before beginning to explore the possibility of multiple SELVES tested against multiple (past) REALITIES.

NOTES

[1] These remarks from WORMWOOD REVIEW. Issue 59, p. 99. 40 DAYS, APPLE NIGHTS was published by Morgan Press in Milwaukee.

[2] No pagination in book, poems referred to solely by title.

[3] "Inland Maine."

[4] "Enough."

[5] "Getting Into Bed Early With."

[6] "Here There's Just."

[7] "no i don't want the...."

[8] From December 11, 1980 tape.

[9] Title first line of text: "Thinking of What A...."

[10] Again the title's the first line: "Drifting the...."

[11] "All the Women Poets I Like Didn't Have Their Fathers," no pagination.

[12] *Ibid.*

[13] "Sometimes It Still Seems Like Before."

CHAPTER X

OLD HOUSE POEMS was published in January, 1975 as 28 in the Capra Press (Santa Barbara) Chapbook Series.[1] We're still—like in THE OLD HOUSE ON THE CROTON—in colonial times, only on the coast now, and involved no so much with individual lives and perceptions as with a melancholy, devastating sense of the sweep of Time. It's ZEIT UND SEIN tied to The Image, really, a concretizing on the Heideggerian vision of Time as the underlayer of all reality.

Like the last poem in the book, the contrast between underlying (real) time-*flow* ("sun thru this dotted/swiss catches the/ rows of copper//rainbow on the/ceiling on the/floor") and the human (mis-)perception of permanence in the midst of this flow:

>..........the
>
> girls ruffling
> clothes tasting
> bread   laughing
>
> in this tiny
> alcove as
>
> if they
> always had.[2]

Or back to poem 12 in the Harlow House sequence:

> When you don't
> look things
>
> unbraid   bones
> in the garden stop
>
> being bones
>
> Sea eats the voices[3]

Any sense of human permanence is eaten away, corroded, swallowed, devoured. Man may *see* himself as permanent, may expand inside the illusion of solidity and substance, but it remains only illusion.

As in THE OLD HOUSE ON THE CROTON poems, threads of war, economic-disaster, tragedy Out There run through the weave, but here they're at a one-step of further "remove" from immediacy/concreteness. Here we don't so much have people being taken through their time-paces, as Time itself on the move through stationary, vanishing humanity:

>women in silk
>placing shells
>under glass with
>the pressed
>flowers   hardly
>
>hearing the sea
>the rumors more like
>something gone
>before   be
>longing to another
>time   some
>thing written on
>snow with snow[4]

Time is imperious here, takes on a life-form-vitality of its own. It becomes aggressive, like some sort of alien force:

>She wakes up   smoothes
>her hair   it seems
>
>as if the mirror
>was waiting for her
>to join her
>reflection[5]

Read: to join her "ancestors"/her "dream of who she is"/the "idea that she is" proceeding from the Mind of God.

In fact isn't this whole book written as if it were a drama inside the eternal pastless, futureless MIND OF GOD? As if the people (*and the places!*) were all dreams in this divine mind?!?!

> high on this
> june   on dreams
> of fleets his
>
> unborn son will
> take over never
>
> supposing how
> the knocker will
> shake the house
>
> when other news
> comes[6]

Notice how nothing stays fixed/in place, everything dissolves, refuses to fix on any stable form. Talk of money dissolves "like old rope" (p. 23), silver turns "into some/thing else" (p. 22), walls "blacken/around the edges" (p. 23), wall paper blurred before a woman's eyes (p. 25), life itself compared to unravelling yarn:

> waiting   staring
> thru small panes
> of glass fixing
> the room in her
>
> blood how other
> snows might have
> been spent
>
> sewing in it
> feeling as if
> her life was
> yarn and the
> yarn was
> unravelling[7]

The inanimate, infused with this sense of time's unravelling, takes on a will of its own: "threads in the hem/of her dress fraying//unravelling as if to put down roots. . . ."[8]

OLD HOUSE POEMS are really only one step away from a Science Fiction nightmare where passive Time suddenly becomes active and takes on a will, decides to undo/unmake/dissolve The World.

It's difficult to find poetry anywhere in which Time is more actively devouring, in which the whole world of symbols all revolve around this one anihilating event. The sea eats "the sun" (p. 20), ashes, almost in revolt/willingly blow "back into/the room," and branches scrap "the moon/with icy antlers" (p. 41). Everything is filled with baleful, inner life ("schrimshaw with a/ strange woman's face/out of it . . ." (p. 41), and at times the anihilation reaches out and achieves cosmic-sweep, we're suddenly thrust into the time-mechanics of light-years, dead-stars whose lights to us still seems alive:

> . . . . under a
> moon of an old whaling
> ship like that
>
> ship navigating by
> long dead stars[9]

The faceless, anonymous characters in this Time-Anihilation drama sometimes quake with fear as the perception of Time-Reality seeps in on them. Like the woman who talks too much

> . . . . because
> she's afraid
> of silence
>
> lies down on
> the damp floor
>
> lets the quiet
> fill her[10]

Quiet is death, silence is suicide, stopping allows Time to invade and cancel you out.

Human-life in this larger Time-Frame assumes the stance of self-delusion, the pretending that things last, that continuity and extrapolations in the future are possible.

On the edge of the Civil War the then-inhabitants of this old house in Plymouth have their portraits painted, bodies first, then heads, only all that gets painted is the bodies.

> . . . . let the
> painter come
> paint bodies all

> winter as if
> everything would
> still be calm when
> he came around in
> the spring to
> do the heads.[11]

Only when spring comes war comes with it "like a/stone hurling/toward a mirror."[12]

The force of the mirror-image here is particularly strong because of its tie-in with a whole mirror/glass leitmotif that runs through the book that is *the* image-comment on the quality/flavor/savour of the lives that "flow" through the houses themselves.

The houses' inhabitants never really are *inside* Time/the Time of Their Lives, but see Life reflected/second-hand/hinted-at/guessed-at, never grasped or digested.

In Poem 4 in "The Old House: Plymouth," there's an iris in a vase near a mirror in which black lines are starting to spread in the corners "like/a woman's veins//behind her knees," in Poem 5 we're told there are "so many mirrors/for one room," immediately followed by "women in silk/placing shells/under glass . . . hardly hearing the sea," in Poem 7 "mirrors stop/reflecting gold" and a woman's brother sails for Spain, Poem 8 has "mirrors pushing/down to the//floor," in Poem 12 the frightening essence-dissolving image of the mirror takes on its own hungering life: "smoothes/her hair it seems//as if her mirror/was waiting for her/to join her/reflection. . . ." The equation hinted at here is that the indirect reflection of life in mirrors is the same as human life-reflection. Perception equals reflection. Low-humming, muted Awareness never pieces inside the real (tragic) dimensions of Time-In-Movement.

In Poem 22 of the Plymouth poems there's a particularly revealing image. We're in a child's room full of dolls, all different kinds of dolls, ragdolls, stonedolls, wooden dolls, you name it. The child's gone, a latter-day visitor comes in and is "pulled into the doll's glass eye!"[13] As if . . . as if . . . the doll's eye, like the mirrors, merely conceal another Reality of Seeing, God-Time just inside/behind things, watching the intrusions and decays of Human-Time. Look how Poem 22 ends! The glass eyes of the doll have "devoured" a visitor . . . followed by:

> .... leaf
> outlines in the
> coal of her blood
> becoming the green
> leaves again,

which takes us back through biological into geological time, replays (backwards) the dovetailing transitions from green to coal and back again linked to the composition of our blood/emotions. We're dwarfed in the immensities of the time-dimensions that flow around (and through) us.

Really, with all its prismatic glass- and mirror-games, the OLD HOUSE POEMS are much less "tactile," much less "here," than their THE OLD HOUSE ON THE CROTON analogues, and represent a failure to get *inside* past reality, instead represent a heightening of awareness of the time-journey itself. Lifshin here never quite makes it into the consciousness of these houses/the people who inhabited them, but stays outside in the envelope of Time that surrounds (or better yet "surround*ed*) both them and her.

The OLD HOUSE POEMS represent a critical breakdown in Lifshin's attempts at ego-projection out into alternative worlds. Protoplasmically searching out alternatives to a Buckowskian now, in MUSEUM she's taken on the garb of Amerindia, in THE OLD HOUSE ON THE CROTON attempted with some success to project herself into the concept- and sense-envelopes of colonial America, here the OLD HOUSE POEMS are attempts to expand the territory of this same colonial world, meeting face to face, instead, with the very vehicle/media/mode of the attempt itself—the viscous, corroding fluid of TIME. She becomes a worldless identityless "wraith," disembodied and displaced, looking for a space and an epoch to call her own. The question is "What alternatives *can* be left for her, and how does her next volume, UPSTATE MADONNA, serve as probe-mechanism in this quest?"

NOTES

[1] Two poem sequence in book, "Harlow House" (15 parts) and "The Old House: Plymouth" (35 parts). In a note dated May 21, 1981, Lifshin writes: "Harlow House is in Plymouth, Massachusetts, is colonial, but tho I did take the time to read pamphlets about it, all that dissolves. I was aiming at emotional accuracy, not history—tho the dates and names are probably accurate."

[2] *Ibid.*, p. 52.
[3] *Ibid.*, p. 14.
[4] *Ibid.*, pp. 21-22.
[5] *Ibid.*, p. 29.
[6] *Ibid.*, p. 28
[7] *Ibid.*, p. 26.
[8] *Ibid.*, p. 27.
[9] *Ibid.*, p. 42.
[10] *Ibid.*, p. 47.
[11] *Ibid.*, p. 49.
[12] *Ibid.*
[13] *Ibid.*, p. 40.

CHAPTER XI

UPSTATE MADONNA, POEMS 1970-1974,[1] like 40 DAYS, APPLE NIGHTS, is out of sequence with Lifshin's linear development, but at the same time has the psychological function of regathering forces, reexamining identities, regrouping possibilities before continuing on in her poetic-psychic I.D. journeys.
It's divided into four sections, "Biography," "Middlebury Poems," "People & Places" and "Driving Home," and it serves as a solid summing up of Lifshin up to 1974.
The first poem in the volume, "Men Anything She Can Pull Around her Shawls She" is crucially placed as a kind of entrance-hall into the Lifshinian psyche and reveals her exactly as WRAITH SEEKING A (ANY!) I.D.:

> SHE
>
> keeps things between her
> self and other people
> hair   the blank
> words of a page
> she says she sleeps
> with everyone so
> you won't know
>
> wraps those words
> around her like some
> one else's mink and slits
> the phone   when she
> was young she squeezed in
>
> to tight rubber girdles
> waited behind a science
> contest study of the
> eye   now the
> glass in front of her
> eye goes deeper
> in than you can see

> when she reads or at
> a party she dissolves
> inside clothes that
> can fool you for
> days   she doesn't
>
> believe in the stars
> but her sign is the
> crab and her house is
> on her shoulders
> most of what she sees
>
> is like someone looking
> out of some place
> underwater where light
> is something that twists
> thru dark layers like
> something you half
> remember waking up[2]

The quintessencial Lifshin! Always keeping "things" between herself and The World, self-knowledgeable enough to see her HAIR, her POETRY, even her self-generated MYTH OF SEXUAL PRODIGALITY as so many screens/filters. Again the honest admissions—words are "showoffy" ("some/one else's mink"), she's always been vain, deepsea hiding-image of the Poet on the Run, seeing reality prismatically twisted by the distorting powers of her own escaping mind. The Out There remains Unreal and the principle function of all poetic systems is escape-dissimulation.

Certainly this is true of LIFSHIN IN THE WORLD when poetry doesn't function (as it does in identity-travelling) as deep reality PROBE, but dually as CONFESSION (between herself and page) and BUNKER (between herself and The World), because the fact is that, although she *says* her game is subterfuge and dissimulation, the fact is that, although she's exploring nothing NEW, there's never been anyone more confessionally honest than Lifshin facing herself prior to facing the Out There.

It's interesting to see here how she automatically rejects The Past. One voice says FIND YOURSELF IN THE 'THEN,' another bounces back PENETRATE INTO THE 'NOW.' At Chartres she's attracted intellectually by the idea of medieval unity, but,

> . . . my eyes drift
> from the paper
> to the last leaves
> catching in mouths
> of other trees. . . ,[3]

a referencing back to Nowness that's repeated again in "I'll Say Monet the Next Time" which is perhaps her fullest single statement of Bergsonian Nowism:

> to see properly
> is the hardest thing
>
> he did the same
> scene over and over
>
> to see properly
> the way what
> ever moves
> has a this-ness
>
> you can touch[4]

And this "thisness" in Part 3 of the same poem almost becomes the Face of God doesn't it:

> feel of stone
> eaten by sun
>
> something just
> at the point of
> becoming light
> on the water
>
> making the water
> most itself
>
> as it becomes
> something different.[5]

That "something" inside Reality makes things what they are/gives them individuality, is the identity-giver/reenforcer, a transcendent creative FORCE right out of Lifshin's family tradition of "presencing" the Divine inside the everyday.

The closer Lifshin gets to the banal/old-hat/everyday, paradoxically the closer she gets to The Mystical. It's as if all the flights into alternative mysticisms have been unsuccessful escape-attempts from a mystical reality she began with and to which she inevitably returns.

The conflict that runs through all these poems is the conflict between Poet as Self-Promoter/expressor and the World as Conformist-Maker. The idea of "thisness," the Scotisian-Hopkinesque concept of "haeccitas" or "inscape"/*individuality* is a constant here. The world moves to distort and mock, the "presencing" poet lights to find her own divine self somewhere inside where her divinity meets the hidden divinity underlying reality. Take "Hair," for example, everyone's out to change her hair (world-conformity) only she resists until she finally comes to the revelation that:

> what grew out of
> the dark where i
> couldn't reach
> like dreams or
> poems was beautiful
>
> shouldn't be
> squeezed into
> changed into
> something different....[6]

Here in UPSTATE MADONNA she develops the revealing metaphor of the Two Eves, one Eve the normal, socially-acceptable cardboard "hypocrite," and the other, the Night-Self, the Eve of the Psychic Time-Trips, who remains secret, revealed only to herself and her private poem-world.

Cocteau-film-style, the Mirror here becomes a door between the dual Eve-worlds: "The dream of the letter I'm writing you/ or people moaning/repossess and the/mirror i walk into/trying to leave my/clothes on the other side...."[7]

The *classic* statement of this split two-level Day and Night Self, though, is a poem that appeared in the VAGABOND ANTHOLOGY, "This Other Her Running, Dissolves":

> sometimes when i
> eat the crusts of
> things i don't want
> or hang up the phone

> i smell her smoke
> Men who've touched
> me have tasted the
> dark apples of her
> brain i don't
>
> know if anyone can
> love her. her clothes
> smell like my clothes
> then there were those
>
> mirrors i could hear
> her talking in them
> hear what she said
> to her men moving
>
> by touch just out
> of reach a voice
> in the desert fading
> out sometimes tho
>
> i wake up with her,
> almost afraid it's
> like half seeing
> something hair
>
> a nipple thru
> the thinnest silk[8]

The perfect image isn't it? The socially-acceptable self suffering the pangs of conformity-induced hypocrisy versus the messianic-mystic ("voice in the desert") self that simultaneously is saint and ("a nipple thru the thinnest silk") sensualist.

There's another poem in this volume (also originally published in VAGABOND, later part of the VAGABOND ANTHOLOGY) that makes this whole conflict much more understandably "everyday." Out of the mythic to the daily-bread level. Title: "The No More Apologizing The No More Little Laughing Blues." Point: there's one Wyatt-reading, dream-writing, gypsy-haired narcissistic ("i finally loved my legs"), child-shunning, practically sexless but longing-for-sex/love woman who is hidden inside The Model Housewife, The Model Daughter, The Model Citizen.

She wants to PLEASE, above all, to PLEASE, fit in, make

no waves. And all the time there's this OTHER subterranean Henry Millerish Self that's not only crying for expression but that (even hidden) keeps developing:

> the A the star the good girl
> on the forehead   the spanking
> clean haunted half my head
> but the poems had their own life
>
> and my life followed where the poems
> were growing   warm paper skin growing
> finally in my real bed....[9]

The conflict is at the same time shattering and healing. The very fact of the necessity (or at least imagined-necessity) of subterfuge allows the underground vault gardens (the image here is ant fungus) to grow extravagantly. Because the question remains CAN ANY POET EVER LIVE IN HIS INSIDE THE MIRROR COCTEAUIAN POETIC IMAGINATIVE POETWORLD FULL TIME...?

Isn't Lifshin's answer in another poem, "Blue Water":

> tho poems grow
> like mushrooms
> all night?[10]

Everything seems pushing her toward "escape." The realm of Night takes on a variety of forms, the Dark Eve takes various trips, assumes various forms. In the "Middlebury Poems" (pp. 59-76) she travels with the Indians again:

> .... charred
> stones   arrowheads
>
> a bowl made of stone
> not found in new england
>
> men   iroquois travelling
> close to water kneeled
>
> hear the rushes grinding
> corn in that stone....[11]

She relives the whole colonial White-Indian encounter again, the White-Man nightmare of digging in, asserting territory and then the Indian-attacks: "this time they came on/friday when the men were//in the field//... men moving thru//the kitchen like a bad dream."[12] Special interest here, of course, in the Situation of Women, and again the same floating, dreaming sense of unreality," as if the women in the poems, the colonial, "projected," imagined, recreated women hardly understood who-what they were:

>................ one
>
> mirror pulled from
> mud   its frame
>
> rotting   but the
> glass showed the
>
> dazed eyes of a
> woman who still
>
> couldn't understand.[13]

Here in these "Middlebury Poems" we find even more of the bafflement and frustration with The Past that we found in the OLD HOUSE POEMS. Sympathies remain with the Out There; the Indian Past sang for Lifshin, but this white colonial past is a vision of self-destructing to which she applies her old standby vision of dissolution, dissolving, disintegration, as if dissolving-Lifshin, on a time-trip back into a possible-past *wishes* the past dissolved so that there's no way or reason for her to attempt to return to it again:

> the current   the
> water eating them[14]
>
> rooms like a
> museum even
> then   listening
> for ghosts[15]
>
> .... men
> bailed out the water
> with their shoes
>
> fragments.   businesses
> that failed   the lots
> getting smaller

> even the tough pine
> roots dissolving.[16]

There's a finality here isn't there in viewing the Whiteman tenuously hanging on to the New (Indian) world and then being forced to let go. No sympathy, really, but rather a large, heavy sadness, no praise-poems or fascination-poems, even exploration-poems the way she was still exploring in MUSEUM and OLD HOUSE ON THE CROTON, but lamentations, dirges, locks turned, worlds turned away *from,* not the house dissolving here but a whole colonial experimental world.

Really the most important section of UPSTATE MADONNA—almost a textbook in perception—is "Driving Home" in which she sets up herself as a Sub-conscious Cavern-World Impressionistic, Fine-Tuned YOGA:

> i drift with
>
> the poem you
> sent into an
>
> underground
> river where
>
> indians eat
> fish so old
>
> they had no
> eyes. if i
>
> shut my eyes
> i hear the
>
> water that
> flows under
>
> the columbine....[17]

Revealing the superimposition of Indians (again) and eyelessness . . . or (more accurately) *perception beyond eyes,* the way she herself begins to perceive: "When i touch/the chair i hear/bluebears that//were wild in its/leaves when there//were red flowers in its branches."[18] She goes back to the origins of things, sees Reality as Flux and Development and can go upstream on their developmental trajectory, trace them back to

beginnings/essences.
Fingers become eyes:

> .... the light gets
> nearer, i can taste
> it on my fingers[19]

She beings to feel the movement of things in terms of large energy-blocks/-waves: "... the/water moves/dark between the/ snow dunes... pulling light/around the/black stones."[20]

Her perception becomes psychedelic; instead of trying to mould perception into a coherent, "civilized" whole, she begins to accept it/*herself* as fragmentary, as sensitive as milkweed puff-seeds:

> .... the poems are
> fragments are pieces   i've
> been wanting them to
> connect the way
> i've been wanting my
> life to. But it's
> all milkweed[21]

In fact nowhere else in the Lifshin Canon is there such a sense of celebration as in "Not Thinking It was So with Yellow Flowers":

> when I woke up
> I thought it
> wasn't true
> the air was so
> bright and
> yellow flowers
> were falling
> from the pepper tree
> like suns[22]

Pantheistically, joyously optimistic, this is Lifshin at her optimum belief that the Presences behind things are "benign," a *radical* polar opposite from the other dread-sensation that emerges in her most pessimistic poem, "Dream of the Dread Bird":

> a dread bird
> sits in the
> black walnuts
> he's been there
> a lot lately
> his beak splits
> the moon   his
> feathers on my
> pillow   i can't
> breathe   forget
> my arms wrapped
> tight to stop
> his claws like
> a woman who
> just touches
> her own breasts
> feels for lumps[23]

Hasn't she "cosmologized" The Male here, the Dread Bird not GOD, as one might first think, but The Male that runs through UPSTATE MADONNA and many of the other (earlier) poems, the Male that splits the feminine Moon?[24] And doesn't this male "presence"—not the Presence of the Divine in Nature, but a Peer-Presence, an equal and negative same-level Presence—impinge on one of the psychophyical centers of her femininity ... the breasts?

The Anti-Male reaches a peak in UPSTATE MADONNA; the Madonna-image itself becomes a kind of militant SHIELD. The Male becomes violence, a Death-Principle:

> .... he hates
>
> his penis   wants a
> woman who can make
> it do what it cant
>
> some pretty slut to
> give up all cocks
> for him   what he'd
>
> really like is a
> woman with long
> black hair   her wet

> slit open on his
> fender like a
> dead deer.[25]

It's all "control" here isn't it? The Principle is CONSCIOUS CONTROL that disallows The Poet to slide into and stay inside the UNCONSCIOUS/UNCONTROLLED.

Poem after poem says the same thing:

> "Holding On" (pp. 94-95)—Young woman controlled by a man, model brutalized by The Male,
>
> "Fat Thighs & 30 Dollar Eyes (for Bonnie)" (p. 98)— Local whore type who opens her thighs for everyone knowing "that nothing anyone/can touch about her/is real,"
>
> "The Man Who Turns Everything to Shit" (pp. 82-84)— Totally devouring (shit-converting) man who trashes everything he touches: ". . . he wants every/thing that isn't/his . . ." (p. 84),
>
> "Stone Soup Leaves" (pp. 34-39)—Another dominator, scoffer, controller: "he got jealous of what/ever i wrote down" (p. 38).

The theme that runs through all these Man-Poems is uncanningly the same: ESCAPE FROM CONTROL. As if once she'd really found an independent artistic,wildwoman, night-fantasy Eve-Self, she couldn't backtrack into the hypocrisy of being Adam's RIB again. She reaches back into the earlier Lilith-Layer, Woman Self, not Other-Controlled, always reaching out for the yellow pepper-tree flowers falling like suns, the Perceptive-Creative High, the experiential merging with the Powers inside Reality.

All in all UPSTATE MADONNA is an excellent summing-up of Lifshin up to the 1974-5 period. We get biography, a touch of time-projection ("Middlebury Poems"), a good solid sense of her Selfness in relation to a wide spectrum of social "controls" (especially The Male) . . . and to top it off we're allowed into the eyes of Lifshin the Ecstatic, the Vangoghian post-impressionistic mystic whose perceptions swim headily in the existential currents of The Divine.

NOTES

[1] The Crossing Press, Trumansburg, New York, 1975, the first *major collection* of Lifshin's work.
[2] *Ibid.*, p. 11.
[3] "Thought of Faces On," p. 12.
[4] *Ibid.*, p. 14.
[5] *Ibid.*, p. 15.
[6] "Hair," p. 24.
[7] Poem title "The Dream of the Letter I'm Writing You" flows right into the poem itself, p. 32.
[8] THE VAGABOND ANTHOLOGY, ed. John Bennett (Ellensburg, Washington, 1978), p. 179. My remarks on this poem in my anthology POESIA TAMBEM E LITERATURA/POETRY IS LITERATURE TOO— (Florianopolis, Santa Catarina, Brazil, 1980), p. 86—are apropos here: "The 'dark apples of her brain' image here is perhaps the key to overall meaning; Lifshin is two Eves, a daytime, 'acceptable' Eve, and another nighttime 'unacceptable' Eve. It's a schizophrenic theme that runs throughout her poetry —the conflict between her 'real' self and the self that society expects her to be. . . ."
[9] *Ibid.*, p. 42.
[10] *Ibid.*, p. 26.
[11] *Ibid.*, p. 59.
[12] *Ibid.*, p. 66.
[13] *Ibid.*, p. 70.
[14] *Ibid.*, p. 73.
[15] *Ibid.*, p. 75.
[16] *Ibid.*, p. 76.
[17] "New Hampshire," p. 107.
[18] *Ibid.*
[19] "The Light," p. 108.
[20] "Blue Sleighs," p. 109.
[21] "Wildflowers, Smoke," p. 111.
[22] *Ibid.*, p. 123.
[23] *Ibid.*, p. 117.
[24] It's important to note the emerging Madonna-image here that Lifshin will continue to use . . . with all its moon-association overtones.
[25] "The Way He Is With Woman: Or, It's Always Show and Tell with Him," p. 85.

CHAPTER XII

PAPER APPLES[1] is a summing-up volume like UPSTATE MADONNA but on a much reduced size. Marvin Malone, the editor, though, with all his usual uncanny perceptiveness, does give us poems that splice/combine/melt themes and currents into single wholes. Like:

> HIS RELATIVES
>
> look at me like
> there's something
> wrong with what
>
> no table in the house yet   just
> rooms full of
> huge leaves
>
> cats and stones
> instead of dust
> mops   the books
>
> piled to the sky
> light could be
> roaches it's
> 6:00 and all i've
>
> made is a
> poem   stoned on
> the light how it
> falls thru the
>
> quince trees
> in this dark
> house without

> a rug i seem strange
> troublesome as
> an atypical cell
> you have to watch[2]

Lifshin as Outsider/Anti-Housewife contrasting domesticity and ecstasy, all in a context of Cosmic Evil ("atypical—read 'cancer'—cell") that implicitly ties in with the control-mechanisms of Wife/Thrall in a Male Force-Field. She wants to be the Pure Ecstatic, to secrete poetry, only here comes The World, his relatives, trying to force her into a workaday world.

Or the WHY behind the dissolving-house syndrome:

> as you know the
> houses i live
> in dissolve are
> like snow legs
> in a blizzard
> less real than
> the houses i
> sat around in
> stoned on the
> lives of other
> women   i'm most
> comfortable with
> ruins   rings the
> bones in back
> of glass   after
> i write poems
> i learn to do
> what happens in
> them and know
> as soon as i
> don't want some
> thing i can
> have it[3]

Her house, *her* life unreal . . . when contrasted with the houses/lives of Others. The disease of Total Empathy. And then the being more comfortable with RUINS, the already-over, the broken, emptied-out . . . so she as Creator can enter in and FILL THEM. You can see the problem as sociological *or* artistic. As

Creator-Poet she prefers worlds that she can complete, shuns the places that leave no room for her shaping-, moulding-, forming- faculties. Comfortable with RINGS—the feminine. And the "bones in back of glass"—read the lingering traces/echoes/remnants of The Past. Glass here equals mirror; again by bouncing her image off herself she can project into/create other, previous lives. The poem precedes/creates The Reality. And then the most revealing of all, the relationship between her Will and The Possible: "(i) know/as soon as i don't want some/thing i can have it...." Which is THE declaration on Total Detachment—only by losing can you gain, only by dying can you have eternal life. Call it the paradox of the Liberated Will: wanting cankers acquisition, the role of the Poet-Creator is to submerge herself negatively into The World and thereby both become and (re)create it.

As Poet-Creator she doesn't need The Real, sits—in fact—inside her own creation removed as far as possible from any collision with Realtime/Realcontact:

>..... i made up
> the lovers in
> all the poems
> called wednesday
> know what does
> not happen is
> what makes the
> poem and don't
> want this to
> be enough[4]

WHAT DOES NOT HAPPEN IS WHAT MAKES THE POEM! In other words, poetry becomes alternative-world CREATION, serves as a kind of psychological steadying-mechanism, a psycho-gyroscope, a defensive mind-construction mechanism, filling in the blanks, isolating and insulating against LACK.

The poem is alternative-reality, and also MASK: "this is a poem to/the people who think/i've been direct with/them...." It's not really a *question* of being or not being DIRECT, but both hiding *from* the Out There and burrowing *into* THE TOTALLY INDEPENDENT LIFE OF THE MIND/IMAGINATION.

I think she blames herself too much here:

> . . . this is a poem to
> the people who think
> i've been direct with
>
> them it's for the men
> who thought my legs
> opening said what i
>
> wanted. . . .[5]

It may be true that she "wanted to hide [some poems] even//before [she] knew they were [her]," as if the HER that hates/rejects/hides *should*, by some cosmic law of wide-spectrum benignity, love all, accept all, welcome all, even if it's destructively stalking her, but balanced up against this much-too-elevated self-expectation, this heroic sense of cosmic benignity, she *does* face The World as Enemy. In fact this is one of the major "areas" covered in PAPER APPLES—the necessary why that *creates* the split between The World of Grinding, Everyday Reality and the unhampered, soaring world that SHE creates as Imaginative Cosmos-Shaper.

There's a generous selection of poems here dealing with (male) violence:

> he said he did
> not recall the
>
> rapes   the
> killings 7 in a
>
> few   not till he
> pieced things to
>
> gether   i'm very
> good at that i
>
> never knew their
> names   i'm
>
> telling you be
> cause i'm living
>
> on borrowed   i
> don't know

> what's true
> what isn't
>
> if i had   i'd
> have told before
>
> they kicked me
> between my legs[6]

The WHY of dissimulation/screen/mask. How else can she face irrational killer-reality except escaping? Although in the key-revelatory poem, "Shopping Bag Anna," she *does* come up with an alternative to dissimulation—*counterattack*. Anna, the grandmotherly battered wife, reacts to brutality:

> . . . . after
> a few sobs she told
> how he'd been
> boozing   punching
>
> her around   i went
> and got a hammer
> anthony's last earthly
> words were "oh my
>
> head". . . .[7]

Shopping Bag Anna dismembers Anthony's body and distributes his body throughout Chicago on eight separate trips.

The pacifist-vision *never* satisfies Lifshin. Anna is declared "not guilty," but those (among them herself) who don't fight back? Catch the attenuated despair of *this* image:

> 10 years ago a
> woman let her hair
> hang   he was
> waiting in the
> grey rain, oshkosh
> a poem in his legs[8]

Ostensibly the poem (surface) is about divorce and child-custody, but THE IMAGE IS ALL. Title: Face In a Closet. Hair as rope, something to be hung with/hanging from. And the waiting Threat, the rain. Only Dread doesn't stay small, specific, *even masculine,* does it; it tends to expand its anti-creator ooze out across the whole creation-sky.

There's an important Generalized Dream poem here about a planecrash, with a very interesting misplaced-pronoun game in it that reveals worlds about The Force behind the individual incident:

> It came screaming
> thru the branches
> leaving the plane
> a swayback bird
> sunk in the torn
> house all
> night cutting
> the dead and
> moaning out
> snow falling
> now these
> oranges in the
> bloody snow
> gasoline strips
> of polaroid
> people park
> cars   walk
> up the roped
> streets with
> cameras stand
> in front of the
> twisted tail
> holding their
> children tight[9]

It's not the *plane* that came screaming through the branches, but *IT.* The plane-crash is the result of ITS action—the Death-God Impulse, Killer-"Nature," the devouring force of All-Evil. Behind, under, around her force as Creatrix is this counter Destroyer-Force whose presence hums in the background of everything she does/dreams. Her visionings are always performed against this Other-Force; whatever is self, self-realization, self-expansion . . . flowering . . . is done as a kind of act of defiance against this dragging-down-weight of Cosmic Evil.

To round out the collection here, Malone has included a

number of Indian poems, that in the context of this star-war battle between Good and Evil, take on a different cast and dimension—the ritualization of disaster!

Evil acts, death occurs, only among the Indians Dread doesn't remain vague and "off there" someplace; it is "contained"/fought against by a ritual-context that occidental Lifshin hasn't been given:

> AT DEATH THE CORPSE
>
> was put down about
> 5 feet........ the
>
> corpse painted and
> dressed in the dead
> man's best clothes
> legs bound together...
>
> his clothes and
> clay jars given
> away so his ghost
> won't stay with
> them   his horses
> ridden by his sons
> into the tall grass[10]

Here there is an anthropological "cap"/order/control put on the great Bogeyman of Nature. Very attractive for the secularized Occidental Mind with strong leanings toward re-stating The Sacred. The Sacred, in the context of Amerindian anthropology, removes as much as possible the amorphous fear of a negative unknown that stalks beyond the rim of reason waiting to pounce on humanity.

N. B. how Lifshin dwells on childbirth rituals, puberty rites, focuses on whatever makes transitions/changes/bridges more humane... softer. Like in "Cree Rites," in which "initiation" ends with gifts instead of (The Occident—her experience) anguish, shame:

> ... each woman
> carried some
> of the wood
> home then they
> ate and opened
> suprise gifts[11]

It's not that ultimately The Horror doesn't win. It does. She recognizes that. In fact even within the Amerindian *weltanshauung* IT appears, destroys, devours:

>   looking for water
>   they left the pueblo
>
>   moved to frijoles canyon...
>
>   wove cotton   the
>   sun on their faces
>
>   glazed this clay
>
>   until something with a
>   huge mouth
>
>   moved into
>   their houses[12]

Only the difference here is that the devouring takes place within an ordered, ritualized WHOLE. In fact isn't the lack of ritualization *the* kelson of Lifshin's entire existential crisis? Looking back (and foreward) through her childhood and adolescence and (even up to the Ph.D. orals) into her adulthood and marriage, isn't DIS-order a constant theme, the picturing of the individual being forced to move through time without any sort of sociologically set calendar of events/stages/steps? Order, she's saying, comes from Time Ritualized; disorder is the result of secularized de-ritualization. Hence the fascination with the Shakers that we see in her 1975 SHAKER HOUSE POEMS. The Shakers are "white Indians" and represent a community which has taken the amorphousness of existence and turned it into communal "shelter."

PAPER APPLES, then, is a revealing cross-section of Lifshin's work that shows her as Cosmic Outsider/*étranger*/alien, on the run, on the defensive, fearing the Male and, on a larger scale, what the Male represents—Cosmic Horror/Destruction. At the same time it's a nicely rounded volume in as far as it shows some solutions. It's Lifshin Tortured, though, not—as in the SHAKER HOUSE POEMS—Lifshin Redeemed.

NOTES

[1] Issued as WORMWOOD REVIEW, Vol. XV, No. 3, Issue 59, 1975, this is the mag that has the centerfold bibliography that I've used as bibliographic guide up to here.

[2] *Ibid.*, p. 86.

[3] "Please Send a Short Note a Bio," p. 89.

[4] "Please Send a Short in a Hurry Note Bio," p. 108.

[5] "I Always Wait Till I'm Alone with Paper to Say," p. 96.

[6] "The Third Day the Testimony," p. 110.

[7] *Ibid.*, p. 109.

[8] "The Face in a Closet," p. 108.

[9] The title is (in capitals) "IT CAME SCREAMING THRU THE BRANCHES," which I've "normalized" into the text, p. 109.

[10] Another one of those first-line = title poems: "At Death The Corpse," p. 112.

[11] *Ibid.*, p. 113.

[12] Section xxi of "Thru Blue Dust, New Mexico," p. 114.

CHAPTER XIII

In the SHAKER HOUSE POEMS[1] Lifshin is totally "at home." Here is reality at its most tempered, regulated, sanely "controlled"—no loose ends, ecstacies, yes, but all within the parameters of community/the communal/the "shared," the sharing itself taking on a peculiar twist and rhythm, sexual to a point, and then "distance" is introduced, attraction never allowed to explode into orgasm.

Like in the first poem:

> the first room
> smells like wood
>
> wooden wardrobe cherry
> the wood polished
> plain except what's
> painted blue   blue
> buttermilk pan oval
> box blue bench
> 200 years but
> the fingers that
> mixed powder for this
> blue   the woman
> turning from a
> man's fingers, hips[2]

The naturalness of wood, minimal decoration, 200 years have passed but—echoes of Keats' Grecian urn—the man who mixed the paint and the woman whose dresser was painted never "coupled," never did, never will. It's the aesthetics of permanent, eternal tantalization.

Lifshin doesn't miss a chance to underline Shaker sexual distancing. In Poem 2, in the midst of high admiration for the ordered complexity of the Shaker pharmacopoeia, enter sexual distance:

> ..... pearls of chlorophyll pearls
> of ether
>
> living as brother and sister
> slippery elm compound
> of sasparilla. . . .

Instead of male-female—human!—sex, Lifshin sees the Shakers in terms of some sort of ecological-sexual rapport with the environment:

> fingers deep in the
> moist dark   pulling
>
> Did they talk to the leaves
> as if they were children
> to get the
> largest cucumbers
> the biggest strawberry[3]

It's very attractive, this equilibrium, and its bypasses the primary conflict focal-point in Lifshin's own life—sexuality as irreconcilable, mutually-devouring WAR.

Here in the Shaker world of THINGS Lifshin waxes nostalgic over PURITY. Everything is clean/cleanliness and in the middle of this hygienic obsessiveness with its knife-edge sheet-folds "they/lay down in (them)/alone touch/the smooth white," dream of "a white clean/as new snow."[4] Beyond sex is beyond conflict. Sexlessness becomes a nirvanic state of untroubled joy.

It becomes, in fact, a state of heightened perceptiveness, through the Doors of Perception into the garden of refined, sensitized, almost-psychedelic awareness:

> .... smell of
> wet earth   Stars
> thru the lilac[5]
>
> Men and woman feeling
> light on their backs
> bent their heads together[6]
>
> no one notices the rain
>
> stoned on
> the beauty of wood[7]

It's Joy with biblical precedence, but "purified" of the dross of Lifshin's perennial "sexual invasion" bugaboo:

> sisters dancing to
> god   the men joining
>
> flinging their arms
> and asses   shouting
> for joy   shaking
>
> shaking   didn't
> david and miriam
> dance and sing
> for the lord
>
> some danced so hard
> they didn't know who
> they were where
>
> but they never touched[8]

Fill in the blanks in Poem 8 and you can see the results that flow out of this beyond-sex environment-centered context:

> A place for every
>
> . . . . . .
> did he ever doubt
> that he was in his[9]

A place for everyTHING, and "did he ever doubt/that he was in his," what KINGDOM? CASTLE?, sex (touch) by implication emerging as the chaos-producer, where everything is out of place and The Kingdom becomes Living Hell.

Poem 15 is an abbreviated re-writing of the Genesis FALL story in which the ORIGINAL sin is nicely interpreted as *sexual* knowledge.

It begins in timelessness ("no time on the sundial"), the perfect state of the Pre-Fall, this Shaker/Tess/Hester, one of a long line of knowledge-tasting after-the-fall heroines, is learning the properties/functions/names of the herbs in The Garden: "learning what herbs/heal lemon thyme/sage rosemary//rue. . . ."

She closes her eyes, "lets a man come/closer touch her/lips inside her/thigh," and The Fall is accomplished:

> Slow hot afternoons
> feeling the cool metal desk
> leg   whispering
> about those 2
> who would be
> sleeping in the
> same bed touching
> everywhere[10]

What Lifsthin seems *attracted* by—spinning off the opposite direction from The Fall—is tantalization, sensually-heightened AWARENESS that never quite (Fall-like) breaks down . . . through.

Like in Poem 20 the distanced, heightened sensuality surfaces in Things with only a peripheral relation to sexuality:

> hair undone   alone
> in the small room
> curled with a
> foot warmer
> quilt   pine
> cones burning
>
> writing about
> rubies emeralds
> jade stones she'd
> never put on
> her finger

The life of the MIND/IMAGINATION takes over, never descends into BODY. And—obliquely commenting on her own function as Creator—as long as this aesthetic distancing is maintained, the Artist, with a Hawthornesque aura of "purity" about him[11]—is invested with almost preternatural gifts of creation:

> later afternoon   december the
>
> snow piling higher
>
> cake and spice
>
> women splitting poplar
> wood into sticks
> into shavings

> small carved birds
> for children
> growing in their fingers
>
> bells[12]

She specifically refers to being "entranced with" (stoned on) creation, once "stoned on/the beauty of wood" (Poem 19) and again entranced with threads/weaving:

> dancing with
> linen silk
> with flannel the
>
> threads pulling
> together
>
> Women a
> room of them
> stoned on this
> beauty from
> their fingers[13]

Creators stoned on their creation; and the creation itself only possible within the parameters of strict, sublimated, asexualized CONTROL.

She dwells affectionately on the idea of LIFE AS MONASTIC MACHINE, the Mumfordian concept that the monasteries, in fact, created the "modern" concept of Time, breaking the undifferentiated 24-hour time-FLOW into discreet compartments and functions: "living like wheels in/a delicate machine/they loved."[14]

I wonder, is the sequence causally related between a whole poem on watches and clocks (Poem 12) and (number 13) the actual breakdown of Order/Community, as if (and can this be applied to the monasteries as well?) the introduction of Time/The Modern inevitably cankers and corrodes the spiritual from within, as if The Spirit *cannot* be measured out and controlled without totally breaking down its immeasurable free-flow:

> one day in august
> a class of girls 10
> to 14 suddenly started

> shaking and whirling
> Again in the evening
> Even adults started
> having gift visions
> mansions in the sky
> meetings with strange
> people   dead brothers
> indians   no one could
> sleep or work right....[15]

The divine "shaking" gets so out of control that "they shut/ the door for years." Unknown tongues are spoken—and they too are forbidden. The ID *does* balloon up in the midst of all this order and overpowers the SUPER-EGO. The animal-human overpowers the Dream of ascetic, flesh-escaping DIVINE.

The thrust of the Shaker *ethos* tried to remake *everything*. Poem 14 dwells on name-remaking:

> Changed the names of cities
> hancock   the city
> of peace   its feast
> place mt. sinai
>
> waterveliet: wisdom's valley
> valley of bliss

But even here Lifshin doesn't end on a high-note: "They said they wanted to die in/the body to be reborn//went home with grass stains, starved."

Even earlier in the book (Poem 2), in the midst of all her admiration for Shaker phamaceutical "order," she notes: "but so many pills for/torpid liver sick head/ache constipation dyspepsia."

On one hand Lifshin wholeheartedly thrusts herself into the ordered, sublimated, at the same time religiously ecstatic world of the Shakers, finding there the same sort of ordered ritualization of reality that she found in Amerindia and *didn't* find in colonial America; on the other hand the control-systems here simply don't WORK, the flesh always surfaces, the ecstatic tends (always) to overcome the purely rational. It's the familiar pattern of Rational versus The Beast, and although as Creator-God herself she would like to spin in a distanced sphere of Pure Creative Thought, the human condition returns to pull her back into the rebel flesh and the need to exist in the (imperfect) human community.

Here we're at the heart of the Lifshin psychology, the creative tension between the desert hermit Creator spinning worlds out of herSELF, and the twentieth-century American poet stuck in a secular society that "demands" her to function in, if not *market*, then certainly general capitalistic give-and-take socially "committed" terms.

In this particular Shaker time-trip we see her at her most admiring surrender to an alternative system/world. It's *almost* THERE, and *it*, in turn, gives us the almost-perfect picture of Lifshin's "soul." Sexually-distanced, ecstatic, thing-centered, creation-centered, ORDER-centered, this is the psychological portrait of Lifshin at her ideal/optimum/minimum stress. And what a world of looking-backward insight it gives us: the reason for the torture, the flight, repugnance. She has been functioning at close quarters in the most brutalizing types of guerrilla-action human relations when all along what she *was* was an anchorite immersed in the reality of her own inner divinity.

NOTES

[1] Sagarin Press, 1975.
[2] Again no page-numbering, the poems will be referred to simply by number.
[3] Poem 3.
[4] Poem 4.
[5] Poem 6.
[6] Poem 7.
[7] Poem 19.
[8] Poem 10.
[9] Poem 8.
[10] Poem 17.
[11] I'm especially thinking here of "The Artist of the Beautiful."
[12] Poem 18.
[13] Poem 25.
[14] Poem 26.
[15] Poem 13.

CHAPTER XIV

Does this sound familiar?

>   the dark space
>   in the house
>
>   quiet   useful
>   and plain
>
>   like their lives[1]

It's the SHAKER HOUSE POEMS all over again isn't it, except that instead of wood houses in a (mainly) green setting, here we are among a totally different tribe of ecstatics—the eskimos.

In NORTH POEMS, Lifshin, with ethnological accuracy/ acumen, returns to "the primitive" in a slightly different setting, and admires very much what she sees. There no war, for example, the dread that eventually dominated her American colonial poems never has a chance to even appear here. Not only isn't there any war but "no military organ/no special fighting regalia. . . ."[2]

She doesn't even seem particularly bothered by the fact that "murder occured/sometimes over/a woman," or that "men/ beat their dogs/broke a sleigh," seems, in fact, to almost admire the definitive distancing the eskimos employed regarding violence/the antisocial:

>   The most common
>   way of dealing
>   wihh antisocial
>   acts was to look
>   in the distance[3]

Unexpectedly she stresses egalitarianism. Is that a key to what bothers her in colonial (and contemporary) America, and

also (along with "distancing") what drew her to the Shakers?
The non-militaristic, "simple" eskimos are deftly contrasted with the militaristic, hieratic world of the ancient Egyptians:

> no one knows
> what happened to
> them in the middle
>
> of that winter
> around the time
> that men were
> hauling stone
> toward the sphinx,[4]

implying that *nothing,* at least nothing "different/"radical" happened to the eskimos during the time of the much-trumpeted "peak" of Egyptian civilization. The "long black nights," in fact become dark nights of the Soul; the recluse is lauded and the busy-bee is damned. We're shown the Eskimos with their "carved antlers and ivory" on the one hand, and on the other the slave-state stone-hauling of the Egyptians. Message: blessed are the isolated for they shall see them*selves*!

What I think Lifshin is getting at here is the "smallness" of any tribe's needs, their adjustment to the environment, their "quietness," their "inselved" (enmismado) interiorness, their ability to thrive with a minimum of ballyhoo and noise:

> saucer of oil floating
> a wick of moss
>
> the only heat   the
> nights 50 to 60 below[5]

And this same "smallness" goes along with a certain low-key, "natural" acceptance of, orientation toward DEATH:

> in log tombs
>
> inlaid ivory eyes
> freezing onto the dead[6]

A low, "conserved" profile during life, she seems to be saying, leads to a certain "naturalness" in death. The flow is continuous and it's almost as if she anticipates some sort of reincarnation, a cyclic return to life.

And what is the point of the poem about the old trying to make friends with the cosmos if not that magic and all its ritualistic corollaries arrives at a like (Natural) point of "comfort," that at the same time functions as a taming, a domestification of the force of the Void:

> the old often
> changed their
> names to bring
> summer into
> their bodies
>
> they left warm
> blood in the
> snow for the
> soul in animals
> bones   in teeth
>
> clams or
> quartz crystals
> on a hill shaped
> like a man's
> face so the
> earth's soul might
> be touched
> by sun[7]

There's a touch of the sorcerer's apprentice here isn't there, an appreciation of any system that starts with community/group/clan and then moves out and tries to systematize chaos. Antithetically the worst situation, in the Lifshin world-system, is the individual isolated and at the mercy of this chaos. The primitive anthromorphizes the impersonal, objects are placed on a "hill shaped/like a man's face" in order to draw down the power of the sun . . . and this shaping the world in the image of man in order to draw down the divine, I think, is one of the basic attractions Lifshin finds with Eskimos and the rest of the "tribes" (including the Shakers).

Here the dead don't die. They may even be abandoned, but in their spiritistic magic world, they never die, return as (the neatly-crafted "like foxes' eyes") ghosts:

> numb with snow
> many of the old
> ask for death
> from a son a
> daughter. the
> corpse left on
> the crust   the
> men keep walking
> toward greenland.
> ghosts of the
> abandoned burn
> like foxes' eyes[8]

Lifshin dwells on the Unknown viz a viz the Eskimos:

> . . . . . nobody
> knows how long
> the wall's bones
> lasted[9]
>
> . . . . . .
> Their language is
> thought to be
>
> unrelated to
> any on earth[10]
>
> . . . . . .
> . . . . . when the
> ice retreated
> water ate their past[11]

She stresses their migratory prowess, walking from Asia to Alaska, thin layers of bones and ash in transitory houses en route to some sort of permanence that suggests "no one stayed long. . . ."[12]

In a sense she wants to blot out their origins, make them unique, romanticize them with a sense of wandering nomadicness. After all in the equation of The Egyptians/Pyramids//X/ Wandering . . . they become THE JEWS! She's not saying that the Eskimos are a lost tribe of Israel, gives them their Siberian origin, but she does want to parallel their mystique with that of the ancient, nomadic Israelis. Remember the biblical reference to David and Miriam in the SHAKER HOUSE POEMS, the biblical justification for "shaking"/dancing as praise to the Lord?

> 1000 AD winter
> houses built of
> sod and stone
> driftwood   doomed
> snow houses 60
> could dance in
> Skylights paned
> with stretched
> walrus gut. they
> stretched ropes
> of sealskin: next
> to sex   jumping
> on them was the
> best part of winter[13]

First tribe/community/group with its built-in sense of human "form," its sociological "gel," its fabric of limits and allowances . . . the—still "boundaried"—joy of worship, the reaching out and touching The Divine.

The great irony, of course, is that any sense of physical cold or deprivation hardly enters into the NORTH POEMS. North could be equator as far as actual geography goes; the only geography that interests Lifshin is the geography of spirit contained and at the same time expressed within the insularity of tribe.

Certainly the NORTH POEMS is one of Lifshin's most carefully crafted books. She hardly enters in at all. No propaganda, no real slogans, no ego-trips, just the deeply felt but at the same time objective presentation of an almost-Utopian society traced in its most succinct, sharpest, condensed form. She's come the full circle from the School of Bukowski here, instead of Bukowskianly beginning and ending with ego, starting *and staying* (!) with the reality of An-Other, performing the total switch from Self to an empathetic involvement in an "alien" culture that because of its close-knit clannish supernaturalism, she's able to appropriate and make her own. One would think, in fact, that this is the definitive, "fixed," "finalized" Lifshin, and then we come to the 1977 CRAZY ARMS and realize just how impossible it is to pin Lifshin down to any final identity/form.

In fact there's even a short 1976 volume, SOME MADONNA POEMS,[14] which, although it lacks Bukowski's cataloguing of the every-day, is much more "abstracted," "essential," even "generalized," is still very much Lifshin doing her thing.

At times it's almost as if she's ridiculing her own time-travelling, need/desire to escape:

> AIRPORT MADONNA
>
> is usually departing
>
> lugging 4 heavy
> suitcases and an
>
> air france bag
> of books you
>
> might think she
> knows where
>
> she's going but
> the tickets you
>
> can't see are ripped
> blurred shredded
>
> besides they were to
> a country that
>
> never existed.[15]

At times SOME MADONNA POEMS anticipate the CRAZY ARMS return to self, the battle for total self-possession, against the distorting tuggings and pressures of the world: "she sleeps curled/at night alone/an apostrophe/trying to know/she has to/ possess her/self first...."[16]

SOME MADONNA POEMS is a tentative, peek-show flirtation with the world. Lifshin's not really sure about the ordinary, daily Out There. Is it or isn't it to be fled from, should or shouldn't she yoga into her interior Self?

> CUTIE MADONNA
>
> she doesn't know whether
> to be flattered
> or pissed when she
> drives up to the
> arco and the greaser

> says you're wearing
> musk aren't you
> cutie and runs his
> hand along the
> seam of her fear
> handing her the
> huge key marked to
> the ladies

The Out There threatens, but at the same time she doesn't see herself as passive, nice-guy, VICTIM, but a nasty certainly up to meeting any nastiness the world might proffer here:

> FIBERGLASS MADONNA
>
> looks sweet
> as cotton candy
>
> but gets under
> yr skin give
>
> you the
> slow burn

The Bukowskian desire to SHOCK never quite deserts her here. She's up to the best of them, "walks naked in/front of the/ glass her lawn/hose could be a/cock...."[17]

She *is* profane, sexual, lusty, earthly, game-playing, complicated, a Trickster, but as always there's a kind of shame involved with revealing herself as what she is. The secrecy isn't so much fear as a short of interiorized "retirement," a building of plexiglass walls between her and The Big Revelation:

> .... this
> madonna has a
> secret life salted
> away like coins
> before some war,
> the letter telling
> how to get them
> written in water
> color ink under
> water[18]

The re-assuming of the tough-guy Bukowskian role, at this time-level/-layer, becomes its own kind of escape. You don't excape horizontally into a variety of exotic, "foreign," shamanistic forms, but vertically into yourself. The disguises/stances come from yourself; they're American exotic, taken right out of TV and movie folklore:

> QUARTER MADONNA
>
> takes what you
> put in and
> plays all night

or

> put it in
> and she gives you
> something sweet
> you can eat

She becomes not a Madonna at all, but an anti-madonnaish Kali-Lilith figure, a demonic Wraith right out of the ancient Proto-Indo-Mediterranean:

> DESERT MADONNA
>
> blooms where no
> thing should she
> hoards love like
> water you've
> been on the road
> for days and you
> see her arms
> coming toward you
> but she isn't
> what she seems
> where it matters
> she's hard to
> touch   tough
> she'll get in
> side you and
> leave you burned
> out and dry

She's getting us ready for the CRAZY ARMS horror-film and casting herself as the Arch Svengali, Dracula, the Medusa from Outer Space:

> she wraps her dark
> around you
>
> pulls you down[19]

Although, suprisingly, she ends the Madonna poems with an upbeat romantic touch:

> MULBERRY MADONNA
>
> goes out early
> even before any
> pheasants her
> feet are purple
>
> then later while
> it's still light
> she puts a blanket
> under the mulberry
>
> shaking the branches
> huge pails of
> mulberries purple
> wool purple
>
> fingers and
> that mulberry kiss

It's as if she's assuming various shapes to test out her various selves/facets/bounderies. The time-travelling, after all, isn't HER, it's the INVESTIGATOR, the RESEARCHER, the very act of projecting herself into alternative "objects"/places, also serving as acts of self-negation/-anihilation.

Here in SOME MADONNA POEMS she's playing at the extensions and possibilities of The Total Self. She may *want* to be a Little Goody Two-Shoes, but is honest enough to remove all developmental, environmental, familial, sociological BLAME and say I HAVE ALL THESE POSSIBILITIES WITHIN MY ABSOLUTE ISOLATED SELF, I DON'T NEED PROMPTING.

The Quest for Self never really ends does it? Lifshin finds

infinity inside herself, all contradictions, polar opposites, all heavens and hells. Which is why, when you touch the whole body of her work, you've touched the essential, multiple nature of Everyman.

NOTES

[1] NORTH POEMS, Morgan Press, 1976, no numbering or pagination or titles. I will identify them by first lines. "Model of an eskimo house."
[2] "they lacked true. . . ."
[3] *Ibid.*
[4] "denbigh. . . ."
[5] "the dogs pulling. . . ."
[6] *Ibid.*
[7] "the old often. . . ."
[8] "numb with snow. . . ."
[9] "model of an/eskimo house. . . ."
[10] "inuit meaning/the people. . . ."
[11] "the thule people. . . ."
[12] "following the river. . . ."
[13] "1000 AD winter. . . ."
[14] White Pine Press, Buffalo, New York.
[15] No pagination.
[16] "Madonna of Her Self."
[17] "Madonna Suburbianna."
[18] "Rat's Nest Madonna."
[19] "Root Cellar Madonna."

CHAPTER XV

CRAZY ARMS[1] is a return to "earth" with a vengeance. No exotic tribes, projections into magic spirituality . . . here is Lifshin back in a dream-distorted contemporary America, depressed, writing, "lost." The opening poem, "Depression," in fact, serves as a kind of lietmotif for the entire book, depression solidly fixed inside her "like a huge tumor":

> when i try to sleep
> it presses against
> me   i can't sit
> up like every
> thing was ok
>
> or shop for clothes
> all july i crawled
> down close to the
> ground   i knew it
> would break my
> neck to look up[2]

The whole book has this same dream/nightmare cast about it. It's not so much Lifshin contending with the *real* Out There but is predominantly a battle in the soul, a dream-book, as if the earlier "real-world" Lyn had taken her case to some sort of interior spiritual court and that's where the trial is taking place, an inferno of the soul, a mind-court, ID-battlefield.

Some of the dreams read like R-rated horror-films, lurid, Polanskyan, pathological, like the one in which she goes down into a cellar and finds "two/dead women on the counter/heads sliced from their/bodies no blood its as if//their heads were wrapped tight in cellophane. . . ." The cellophane around them dream-transmutes itself around her, she rips holes in it, and then fears that her fingerprints are on *them* and *she'll* be blamed.[3]

She becomes both victim and assassin, feels herself both as repressed, trapped, destroyed *and* the "suspect" hunted down by the same society that is repressing, trapping and destroying her. The poem ends with an interesting variation on COLD. The eskimo poems are never "cold;" for her cold isn't physical but psychological:

> ...... theres ice and snow
> slamming all night   each day's
> an iceberg   no one knows
>
> the rest   the terrible cold
> down under   something they
> can't begin to imagine[4]

This same revealing connection between The Sexual ("down under") and The Frozen occurs in another poem where the cold-associations pass from disease to sex:

> died of diptheria
> gerald says one night
> the stone room got cold   got cold
> faster....
>
> july   hoarded yr mouth
> your "getting up time
> Lady Lyn" fingers how
> you said the strings
> made them chilly,
> putting them down there[5]

Down there/down under and cold . . . disease. What we're witnessing is the "infantilization" of the sexual impulse; sex as possible connection to the Real (contemporary) World has gone bad on her. Sex means control, misunderstanding, misinterpretation; and so her only viable escape-route (when she's not time-exploring) is back into a Self that becomes increasingly coterminous with The Work.

There are two poems ("After Anne Waldman") which particularly focus in on this problem of "image" misinterpretation, "Woman with A," and "A Woman in a Car Driving."

In "The Woman with A," Lifshin portrays herself as "the/ woman who had/a husband then a/boyfriend like a/child," and gradually builds up details, squishes a little paint on here, lays down a little line there that eventually sums her up as The Classic Outcast:

>   .... woman
> with a reputation
> for being some
> snow lady or
> hot woman in a
> fox and leather
> foxy woman woman
> with a pad of
> paper under her
> skin in love
> with hating
> making up with
> snow in the bed
> trying to write
> yes in it write
> it will be on
> the crust ok
> ok tho her
> fingers burn[6]

It's all contradictory isn't it: cold, hot, loose, tight, free, confined. She becomes a *socially-created* (-judged) symbol, ontologically not flowing out from what she is in herself but *what construct society puts on her.*

Again in "A Woman in a Car Driving" the same social shame repeats itself:

>   ......a woman
> with a reputation
> a marked down woman
> looking for exits...
> ...a woman whose
> life feels like
> a drop of mercury[7]

Her "out" in the face of this sociological outcasting (or, even more accurately, "mis-casting"), is a retreat into Self again.

In "Madonna of Her Self" she images herself as womb-positioning in sleep wrestling with the problem of Self-Hood:

>   .....she sleeps curled
>   at night alone
>   an apostrophe

> trying to know
> she has to
> possess her
> self first....[8]

and interestingly this sleep-exploration is questioning while it simultaineously assumes the FORM of an APOSTROPHE. She seems "lost," but in fact is stationing herself in an attitude of affirmation of The Unconscious/The Creative.

Hasn't she already seen herself as the woman "with a pad of paper under her skin"? Hasn't the (from the outside!) self-contradicting Outcast already associated Bed with Writing: "making up with/snow in the bed/trying to write/yes in it write?"[9]

Writing becomes an alternative universe just as viable and self-contained as any Indian or Eskimo or colonial past, it becomes a territory of self-assertion, a landscape of isolated affirmation—no social context, no anihilating letter A (for Artist?), stigmata, jailing (by definition) of The Free Spirit. If she could only stay in it (the writing) and block out the noises of the so-called real. It's the Artaud Syndrome tugging at her, telling her "Come entirely inside ME" (The Work).

In "The Dreaming of Writing" The Work becomes a scenario for possible alternatives ("lyn he says your/poems are more/real, they know/where they're going"), she even even lies down in them "as if they'll/tell me who i am." But at the end she pulls back:

> .... I'm afraid
> they're to a place
> i can't live yet[10]

So she stops one short step before The Psychotic, lives at the same time in and out of the world, inside the structure of her own work, but still with bridges/webs/catwalks between IT and the so-called Real. There's even one strong anti-solipsistic poem in which she sees poetry not as separate self-enclosed structure but a way *into* The Real:

> i
> want to get out side
> my self i want the
> poems to be like a
> window i can crawl
> out....[11]

CRAZY ARMS, then, is a volume about self-affirmation (possession) in a negative social context of misinterpretation and rigid (attempted) control, and *the* key poem remains "Madonna of Her Self" with its basic affirmation:

>   ..... she has to
>   possess her
>   self first[12]

Only what are the three poems about "Seder" doing tucked in toward the end? We have a mystery here which, when solved, I think goes far in the explanation of why there is so much need for self-affirmation, self-seeking, self-proclaiming *anyhow.* Lifshin's songs of herself, after all, are never Whitmanesquely optimistic and outgoing, but almost universally defensive, angry, "dissolving," "confused." What has happened to The Self that it has been so punished and needs so much buttessing and defense?

The first "Seder" poem begins innocuously enough with an almost-romantic picture of "the moon . . . made of wine." Grandpa ("gramp") is at the end of the table next to the "empty place/for the uninvited guest," Lyn and her sister are in the living room "rummaging/thru velvet . . ."—and now the "revelation":

>   .... rummaging
>   thru velvet in
>   the front room
>   for the matzoh
>   that would be
>   broken   hidden
>   and found for
>   a price like
>   so much else
>   in the house[13]

First broken, then hidden, then found for a price . . . LIKE SO MUCH ELSE IN THE HOUSE! And then in the second Seder poem, to dispel any ambiguity, she openly identifies with the matzohs: "i want to/be skinny dream i/could break off/chunks of myself//hide them under the/velvet pillow like/matzoh that every/one would run to find."[14]

In the third poem this matzoh-Lifshin identification transmutes into matzoh-night ("the night breaking like matzoh") and she ends up "crying under the/table where no one/can see. . . ,"[15] where if you read the line straight through she is ontologically run together with the night: *where no one can see the night. . . .*

The three poems as a unit present us 1). With a male-(grandfather-father-uncles) dominated CEREMONY that 2). Instead of remaining people-centered (Here-and-Now-centered) becomes involved with the personification of symbolic place-functions (the chair for the uninvited guest) and things (the broken, hidden matzohs). She as individual (and female) is somehow ignored. The context is sensuously rich, warm chicken wings, wine, velvet . . . but instead of directing it to her, she feels that somehow she must be "sacrificed" and "hidden" (read ignored) in order to be appreciated . . . and ends up obliquely stepping into the negating role of NIGHT.

She likes the idea of "tribalness" (Eskimos, Shakers, Indians) with all its ritualization of The Sacred which, in terms of conditioning, recalls the ceremonialness of her own childhood . . . but at the same time recognizes that this same "externalization" of behavior depersonalizes and negates the Creative Self.

Two world-views, really, are in conflict here—the Abstract, Combative, Theoretical, Anti-Sensual/-Sensory, MALE and the Concrete, Peace-Making, Practical, Sensual/Sensory FEMALE. In the Seder poems Lifshin is fragmented like the matzohs (with overtones of Christ as Matzoh-Host Victim?), in yet another poem an analogous fragmentation takes place with broken pipes smoked by men talking of war and money:

>dutch family
>bible the
>names fading
>
>blue faded cushion
>cufflinks   hand
>blow bottles   green
>
>bronze blood
>and cranberry
>
>men smoking the long
>delicate clay pipes
>
>talked of war and money

> gunmetal sky
> wind rattling glass
>
> Under this floor
> 1000 pieces of broken pipes,[16]

while her own anti-abstract, totally-evocative mystique concentrates fanatically on capturing/re-capturing THE SENSORIALLY-HEIGHTENED PRESENT MOMENT:

> ....i've watched
> the trillium pull
>
> itself out of the
> mud the red leaves
> turning green   moss
> on the stone   When i
>
> come back thru the
> trees with just the
> moon i'll say your
> name over as a charm
>
> to bring you thru
> the grey birch to
> where you are
> on this page[17]

Her feminism never is political, job- (or even "role"-) oriented, but epistomological. Her world-view is charged with an immediacy of existential freshness, and anything that ascends into the false-heavens of pure speculation, completely turns her off/away. The Seder ceremonies, like any kind of speculative GAME, favors Theory instead of The Personal, and it's this speculative ESCAPISM that she herself is trying to escape from in order to mould her own personal epistomology of Nowism.

Society works in terms of this same theme of anti-human/humane speculation; in fact societal "judgement" is always a priori and completely antipodal to her need to drench herself in "The Real." You can see *why* she needs to create her own independent universe, how, as creator, she spins a selfhood concentrated in the perception and recording of the most subtle shades and variants of her surrounding reality. What she's rebelling against is the occidental tyranny of speculative hermeticism;

what she's reaching *for* is an oriental impressionism that fills out and flavors the sanity of the accessibly near-at-hand.

CRAZY ARMS is a struggle- rather than a plateau-record, Lifshin's next book, WOMEN EARLY PLYMOUTH, is a kind of "letting go," a delineation of *her* territory on *her* terms, a small Paradiso after the painful Purgatorio of CRAZY ARMS.

LIFSHIN & RICHMOND[18] is really a companion volume to CRAZY ARMS, the same kind of excruciating freneticness, anguish, uncertainty, the same "testing" of reality, poems serving as tentative feelers out toward WHO AM I, WHERE AM I GOING?

Sometimes she loses track of The Big Picture altogether and gets totally involved with details, like a Nouvelle Vague camera finding the universe in a grain of sand:

> i'm running
> slamming into
> old houses starved
> for the way light
> eats the worn
> grain of a scooped
> out circle....[19]

But even here she comes back, however peripherally, to I.D., evanesence, the all-human need to leave "traces":

> ... but right
> now with my own
> room dissolving
> i'm starved for
> houses people have
> lived in long
> enough to leave
> what they were
> like fossils
> or pearls[20]

The small details of the world (again like the Nouvelle Vague) are cryptographic symbols of larger concerns, a crack along the porcelain in a wash-basin reminding her of a scratch in a finger which in turn recalls a "crack" in a love-bond:

> You don't remember
> exactly when you
> stop caring for
> someone stop want
> ing his hand on
> you knees but
> the crack wasn't
> there and now
> others are   hardly
> different but
> different.[21]

She's totally alive with poetry; it burns inside her:

> looking down at
> the black snow
> blue angel
> lying down in
> her own snow
> poems burning
> all night
> in her head
> like pots in a
> grove of oranges[22]

It's an ironic kind of juxtaposition, this Richmond and Lifshin back to back. Richmond next to anyone else seems so French decadent, way-out, wierd; here, next to Lifshin, he seems "formalist," very "controlled," a Maker of Poems rather than a vesuvian self-expressionist . . . like her.

Unlike CRAZY ARMS there's next to no concern for "salvation" (self-affirmation). She may—affectionately—complain that her mother is too possessive ("Mama, Let Me Do It Myself") but mainly she's examining her own reality of Crackup, the world outside affirmation or exploration, the world she never really succumbs to, but flirts with, plays footsy with, "gambles" with:

> a broken cat
> the 22 under
> a pillow

> madonna with
> broken zippers
> from rushing too
> fast into
> or away
>
> broken house
> broken window
>
> madonna with
> a gun under
>
> feeling the piece
> of roof falling
>
> a gun in
> side some
>
> wanting but
> not sure if
> she can put
> much together[23]

    Her self-doubt is unjustified. She's not a Sharon Asselin or a Levy or a Wantling; under her Level of Chaos isn't more Chaos, but a foundation of deep, abiding calm.

    She's a caterpillar-sensitive witness to Chaos, sees the old men on a hotel porch successively, slowly disappearing ("the word//yesterday like a/pile of bones,"[24]) sees fatal cancer in others ("He/thought they'd/caught the cancer/early..."[25]), even sees the threat of "anger"/"invasion"/"attack" directed at herself ("if you let it/in every morning/there'll be a/hundred fists/in yr belly"[26]), but the real her, the REVELATION of the real her, doesn't lie in the witnessing of the decline and death of others but in her studying The Supreme Surviver, Martha Graham:

> still beautiful
> still working
>
> high cheekbones
> her hair pulled
>
> back black
> coal eyes

>   black velvet on
>   her shoulders
>
>   no flesh
>   she cant use[27]

It's funny to see how she samples Chaos, feels its Presence to the core, but never (really) gives in to it. It's all part of a testing/probing/exploring of alternatives that she'll never follow. A constant theme in her letters five years after LIFSHIN & RICHMOND is the intrusiveness of her own ballet classes:

> . . . actually ballet is becoming sort of an intrusion i take so many lessons . . . and feel i'm always rushing out to dance. . . .

As she replicates Martha Graham at 81 . . . now 86!

NOTES

[1] Ditto Rations Chapbook Series, #11, Ommation Press, Chicago, 1977.
[2] *Ibid.*, p. 1.
[3] "The I Go Down in the Cellar Dream of Dark Snow," p. 2.
[4] *Ibid.*
[5] "Ghosts in the House," p. 14.
[6] "The Woman With A," p. 16.
[7] *Ibid.*, p. 17.
[8] *Ibid.*, p. 8.
[9] *Ibid.*, p. 16.
[10] *Ibid.*, p. 15.
[11] "She says you know with the. . . ," p. 18.
[12] *Ibid.*, p. 8.
[13] "Seder," p. 25.
[14] *Ibid.*, p. 26.
[15] *Ibid.*, p. 27.
[16] "Philipsburg Manor, 19," p. 10.

[17] "Monadnocks, Tuesday," p. 13.
[18] Bombay Duck, 1977.
[19] "Cape Cod 1972," no pagination.
[20] Ibid.
[21] "Monday."
[22] "High Flying."
[23] "Madonna With a Broken Gun."
[24] "Ole Men Hotel Brenner."
[25] "The Second Second Wife Poem."
[26] "The Angry Blues."
[27] "Martha Graham at 81."

CHAPTER XVI

WOMEN EARLY PLYMOUTH[1] is a plateau-achievement. It's terse, pointed, abbreviated, and represents a *total domination of the material at hand*:

> low tide
>
> tiny black snails moving
> over the flats
>
> fish in the tide pools
>
> mint on her skin   the
> seeds carried
> from leydon
>
> sand burns
> under a nail
>
> grains shifting
> pollen on the water
>
> the sun   her belly
> straining against the
> cloth that keeps
> getting tigher[2]

Objectivistically concrete, with a Symbolist sense of neat, honed image, at the same time Lifshin is eminently human here. She's left herself behind. It's a shift into Time Travel again; and the terminus of this trip is exclusively the colonial FEMALE mind.

As in "low tide," there's a strong sense of "displacement" throughout the book. In "low tide" it's geographical/sociological—the movement to a new land—but as a counter-weight to displacement note the sense of self-containment, self-sufficiency. The woman carries seed from Leydon, and then the seed-imagery is extended, seedlike sand, pollen and then her own pregnancy, a beautifully executed extension of immigrant as seed to immigrant-woman as seed CARRIER.

In WOMAN EARLY PLYMOUTH salvation is self-containment/-sufficiency:

> gulls in the blue air
> a woman watching
>
> frozen salmon sun
> the bristles of
> stiff pine   she
>
> leans close
>
> linseed smell like
> someplace in england
> bayberries like pewter
>
> their sweet smoke
> in her hair   the
> night a necklace
>
> of birds.
> snow   If she
> could just write
> someone this[3]

The purpose of existence here is simply perception and solipsistic self-enclosure in the hum of this perception is very much allowed. You don't have to go anywhere; you're allowed the fullness of perception, sun, pines, linseed, and that exquisitely symbolist image, "the/night a necklace//of birds."

There may be a peripheral, subsidiary looking-backward to England ("smell like/someplace in england" or "blue cabbage. how it ripened/for the fairs/in essex"[4]) but mainly WOMAN EARLY PLYMOUTH is a series of master-lessons in the art of AWARENESS:

> sun on the water
> vetch   blue
>
> berries minnows their
> green fire
>
> shimmering. . . .[5]

It all really becomes "crows pecking at sea weed/*Her* blood filling with sponges," i.e. THE EMPATHETIC ABILITY OF EMPTYING SELF INTO YOUR SURROUNDINGS, BECOMING THE LANDSCAPE. Paradoxically by becoming totally *I* you automatically become totally the Divine Pantheistic OTHER.

Which is why as poetry WOMAN EARLY PLYMOUTH represents a real "high."

Like a comparison between The Dead and quartz-crystals:

> . . . . the
>
> dead grow, quartz crystals
> under the snow. . . .[6]

Or the conjuring up of a late-summer stormy day ("landscape with female figure"):

> the sky
> smokey, lemony
>
> thunder   the leaves
> turning inside out
>
> a woman
> hanging crushed
> roses in the
> doorway[7]

The simple sketching of sky invaded by branches:

> white sky
> branches like
> antlers[8]

The entire volume has this sense of sketchbook succinctness about it. It's a Hopkinesque notebook aimed at capturing the inscape of colonial New England—the "thisness," essence, the inner, essential imagistic core. Everything is subordinated to image, and the image-use is reduced to an evocative minimalism.

Thematically, though, we're on familiar ground—the subordination of The Female by the Male, or (slightly rephrased) the control of the Female by a venal pack of Anti-Human RULES.

And the Scarlet-Letter poem in WOMEN EARLY PLY-

MOUTH doesn't have the loaded-dice justice of a Hawthorne, but ends powerfully, after lashes and whips with:

> her nipples rotting
> on some beach.[9]

The female isn't automatically saved. The dominion of the Rule-Book is mercilessly all-pervading.

Still . . . the integrity, self-ness, self-contained female "vision" remains. Even in the case of a semi-chattel "washing for some/man who isn't hers . . . lives//like driftwood," who, in the face of total external/economic instability, still maintains a strong sense of her own pathway and individualized perception:

> Strange seeds blow
> over the frozen
>
> ground like rice
> at a wedding, *a*
>
> *diary in her blood*
> *writing*. . . .[10]

These early Plymouth women, even under duress, are not so much victims as WITNESSES.

In another poem about The Rule-Book World versus illegitimacy Lifshin's indignation rises to a high pitch. As Witness her protest itself draws blood:

> . . . . Who
> says the crime
> for bastardy   She
> sees the baby
> crushed between
> two other children
> not hers[11]

It's almost as if the dream-monsters from her other books have (time-travelling) come back to invade Plymouth: "The other women/enemies now huge/mouths claws The blood room spinning. . . ."[12]

There's even a return—if somewhat obliquely—to the whole complex of water-images, the dissolving, disintegrating world of The Drowned Lady:

> ....her hand
> pressing between
>
> her eyes. water
> coming close[13]
> ...
> the old woman
> dreams bracelets of
> kelp   ropes
>
> of darkgreen sea
> weed twisting around her sons[14]

Woman in this lost, retrospectively recreated world is not triumphant *in relation to The Rule-Book World*, but only in relation to herself and her immediate environment. The existentialism that Lifshin preaches here is totally personal, interiorized, both literally and figuratively divorced.

In one poem, in fact, the message seems to be camouflage/protective coloration/adaptation to the point of invisibility, all centering around the images of a). A small adaptive fish, the alewife, and b). Frogs hibernating in winter:

> ....learning to wait
> like frogs in iced mud
> moving toward summer
> that quietly. she thinks
> of alewives   silver
> their greyish green blending
> with what's around them....
> She thinks how the
> solitary alewife is
> lost and shuts her eyes[15]

On the surface very "defeatist," self-obliterating, only then comes the counter-question, what is this being-in-waiting waiting FOR? And the answer comes back with a rush of Impressionistic fervor:

> snowflowers thru
> the ice   grey
> moss water
> plants beetles....[16]
>
> cat tails and rain

>   in one room a cloud of
>   smoke and roses...,[17]

Really, what we have here, once we subtract the socio-economic (read Manworld) negatives, is a textbook of "visioning." Given, the women here look back to England, given they are all in a subordinate social role, given the life itself is bone-hard . . . but none of this stifles the visionary impulse to penetrate into and BECOME the world around them.

This is Lifshin's most successful time-trip. She is HERE in all its multi-dimentionality, its sensory capaciousness, richness, fullness. And the feedback message *is* there—NOW, NOW, NOW, NOTHING ELSE BUT NOW, A TRANSCENDENTALIST IMMERSION IN ALL THE FINE SHADES AND OVERTONES OF THE PRESENT MOMENT, THIS IS WHERE THE DIVINE YOU MEETS THE DIVINITY SUBMERGED IN THE WORLD.

At the end of the 1978 collection of her poems, OFFERED BY OWNER,[18] Lifshin has a series of "technique-confessions" that are very useful right here. All these colonial American poems are essentially based on the same methodology of beginning with THINGS and then meditation, projecting back, letting the THING (OBJECT) speak out its essence:

> . . . when I thought I was going to be finishing a Ph.D. in English and writing about Wyatt I read Louis Martz on the meditative process . . . about starting with the physical and moving from that. I went thru the old houses . . . I don't mean to say I went into a trance—but I did try to move back in time, jotted as many notes, physical sensations, qualities of light down. I'm sure some of my own isolation, loneliness and fear got into these poems but it seems right for them. I visited as many of the old houses I could in Plymouth, Mass.—Harlow House, Howland House, Spooner, Sparrow House and the Antiquarian House—pieces of each blow thru here.[19]

Of course *she* is the vehicle time-travelling back to the colonial past, there's no total depersonalization possible, but her sensitivity to the "jeito" of the ambience is marvelously successful, model-techniques flawlessly executed.

NOTES

[1] Morgan Press, 1977, Graphics by Susan Hale Kemenyffy.
[2] No pagination, poems identified by first line.
[3] "gulls in the blue air...."
[4] "sun on the water...."
[5] *Ibid.*
[6] "the winters seem darker here...."
[7] "the sky...."
[8] "earth thawing...."
[9] "can feel his tongue...."
[10] "washing for some...."
[11] "borning room...."
[12] Same as previous poem. The "blood room" referred to here seems to be a special delivery-room ("borning room").
[13] "thinking how he took...."
[14] "shells in the yard...."
[15] "mist in the valley...."
[16] "snowflowers thru...."
[17] "cat tails and rain...."
[18] Natalie Slohm Associates, Inc., Cambridge, New York.
[19] OFFERED BY OWNER, p. 79.

CHAPTER XVII

    Still on the 1977 time-traveller plateau, LEANING SOUTH[1] is Indians, colonial America . . . and Lifshin's own personal past transformed into its own museum stillness/objectivity.
    Apart from the sacred ritualization of life, in LEANING SOUTH Lifshin opens up a bit more as to *why* the Amerindian interest in the first place, a "closeness" that she, the distant, unapproachable Moon Madonna, never seems to find in her own life:

> children were wanted
>
> were always close
> to their parents
>
> skin   even during
> fucking. nobody
>
> put the baby down
>
> except to dip male
> babies in the
>
> wind and snow
> to make them strong
>
> then close to
> the nipple again[2]

    It's not that in her own life (her own family poems) you have any cruelty/overt separation, but the picture that emerges of her mother, her family in general is that of "separateness," a total lack of the kind of flesh-touch continuity she finds here in the Eskimos.
    Referring back to her family there's always the imagery of menace ("the chickenhouse/grows wings/claws settle/on his/ lips . . ."[3]), a feeling of desertion, aloneness, lonely aging:

> She lights
> candles 40
> years, the
> heat turned
> low   Her
> hands are
> nearly
> transparent[4]

The Eskimo world, after all, is ritual that WORKS/FUNCTIONS/IS EFFECTIVE. There may be the same sense of loneliness, "sin," "separateness;" after all the Human Condition doesn't vary, but the reaction to it does. The Eskimos effectively ritualize the exorcizing of evil:

> huge sin must
> have floated down
> to the floor
> of the sea
>
> like dandruff from the
> hair of the goddess
>
> the shaman will have
> to go suck on the
> evil   spit it
> out a pebble
> stone[5]

The Lifshin family world, by contrast, is filled with a ritualization of *angst,* not so much cleansing as anguish-reenforcing:

> by summer
> weeds covered the
> charred hole where
> the store burned
> to nothing, march,
> just after the
> old man died
> my grandmother
> more undone by well
> i know which loss

> and she had reasons,
> all those years of
> watching car lights
> till morning
> In the fall she
> had them paint the
> room white sighing
> about how wood goes
> quickly too as the
> garage sand around
> his blue 53 plymouth
> It was so much
> like ritual[6]

In a sense it's "pseudo"-ritual, isn't it? Not a ritual that objectively rids the world of evil within the context of a community consensus, but a private little act that because of its very privateness, remains hollow and ineffectual. Not ritual, but "LIKE ritual."

Lifshin doesn't want Time secularized, flattened, deprived of its connection to The Divine. When the Eskimo Shaman shamanizes he reaches into The Divine for *advice;* The Secular World is formed, guided, controlled by The Divine:

> everyone falls in
> to a trance   souls
> of animals rise in
> the hut the men
> strain to hear
> what to do about
> their families
>
> where the seal and
> caribou will move[7]

By contrast with this exaltation of the Eskimos with their constant connection to The Divine, when we move (and the juxtaposition into one volume is apt) into the old-houses-world again, for all the raw, evocative technical mastery that Lifshin employs to bring us bodily into the scene, the world remains not tactilly but existentially unreal, not because of any evocative weakness on her part, but because the people themselves who inhabited the houses were unreal for themselves *in their own time.* They were—like Lifshin herself—trapped totally in The Secular, and this limitation secreted an unrealness about their entire surroundings:

> pitch pine,
> stunted branches
> twisting down
> toward its own roots
>
> thickets of small
> grey bones   a
> rusty sleigh
>
> grass blows like
> hair on a girl
> on horseback
> she drifts   dissolves
> in grey wood
>
> becomes the color
> of sky too[8]

When Lifshin herself "merges with Nature" here, she doesn't move into any fulfilling encounter with any "beyond," any greater Power, Force, but, like the Nantucket woman "dissolves," doesn't quite "fit":

> wandered
> wrong in
> the road
>
> i don't
> belong here[9]

And it's easy to see why in poems like "Coming Back to Middlebury" which are precisely about the problem of losing (more accurately "submerging") one's FAITH in a secular world of all-American conformity in which The Jewish was a thing to gloss over to avoid conflict whether imagined or real, instead of totally being what they are, the Jews around her wear conformity-masks. Like the teacher whose fingers "smell of dill but/the chicken liver/dies in breathmints/beyond his anglo saxon name. . . ." They hide their yamulkas in their pants "crushed like some/trojan," and to complete their disguise "most have a/wife named pat or mary."[10]

Only she doesn't stop there in "Coming Back to Middlebury." It hasn't always been flat/truncated/secularized. There was another earlier world in which The Vision still was active/viable:

> ... my uncle
> twists in a bed
> that outlasted
> his mother wakes
> in a quilt from
> another world be-
> fore the cohens
> came and couldn't
> work before jews
> with names that
> sounded french
> came to the college
> wrote music for
> easter and then
> left town fast[11]

She's looking back to "unfettered" Jewishness, self-affirming Jewishness, not camouflaged, hidden, cryptic—and this is a logical route for her own mystical proclivities isn't it, the route of, say, a Jerome Rothenberg or Stanley Nelson, or Menke Katz, a route which, up to now, Lifshin *hasn't* taken.

These three groupings of poems in LEAVING SOUTH have three separate distinct *styles*. The Jewish-exploration poems, the poems that delve into Lifshin's own immediate, personal past, are wry, satirical, totally "rational," no fog, no cloud, no mysticism. She's very able to self-analyze with the most "scientific" of probes, no holds barred, no doors unopened, very Swiftian, Daumier-like. And it's always much the same theme, the negation, forgetting, letting go of a sacred PAST:

> my grandmother was
> forgetting the poems
> she wrote 30 years
> earlier in small
> lines with a green
> pen. ...[12]

The early Americana poems, on the other hand, are impressionistic water-colored capturings of immediate, pan-sensory moments, gliding across touch, sight, smell, taste, bringing the reader into an American colonial past long dead and buried, but still always carrying with it a touch of the grave, mourning, death, and—even more—isolation, strangeness, "uncomfortableness" in a strange haunted present isolated from English/European ROOTS:

> Here dying came like
> blackbirds...
> we bury our dead
> without a moon
> black snow stuffed
> into mouths
> everyone's lips
> numb....[13]

In some ways here in antique America Lifshin's at her shamanistic best. The language is sliced thin, the imagery perfectly turned, carved, crafted. And the message that emerges is that the colonials, cut from their tradition and plopped down in a strange land, never recovered from a sense of existential severing.

Which nicely relates back to the severing of her own roots/Jewishness, an identification between Lifshin as castaway on strange industrialized American shores, and American colonials in a similar estranged, "incomplete," chronically "unfulfilled" state. At least the colonials could merge with a still intact Nature ("we drift too//become those//horses near the/water running . . .[14]), which twentieth-century Lifshin can't do, although at times she tries and the trying usually ends in some sort of existential "straying"/symbolic suicide.

The Eskimo poems are all most scholarly, have a certain lettered "museumness" about them, radiate a breviary sense of sacred texts. They're never satiric, never misty or overhung with an aura of death, but optimistic, positive, "relations" rather than small, perfect oval portraits. Even the supernatural here has a certain naturalness about it. Man is in tune with his spirits, the spirit-SPHERE is simply another layer to everyday living:

> the long dark
> nights punishment

> for killing too
> many animals
>
> their spirits rise
> with the spirits
> of places
>
> ghostly caribou
> in the sky the
> fire[15]

Secularization, after all, means THE DESANCTIFYING, DISUNIFYING SPLITTING OF THE INDIVIDUAL FROM ANY SACRED SENSE OF THE COSMIC "ENVELOPE," whereas with the Eskimos:

> what was inside and outside
> joined[16]

I think her greatest frustration is her often failing, rarely succeeding attempts to join with the "spirits in the hills,"[17] an attempt at transcendental coupling outside of the support mechanisms of tribal context and ritualized conduct-patterns. By being "detribalized" and "deritualized," she's been stripped of the ROUTINE of cosmic "awarenessing":

> The road bleaching out
> behind you in the
> rear view mirror
> where something wrong
> is starting to happen
>
> trailing gas on
> the sand you
> drive the car
> into the desert[18]

This poem inevitably has to come from the I-Lyn Lifshin poems doesn't it? The Eskimo (like the other Indian poems) represent the sacred yogic ideal WAY, the Colonial old-house poems represent WAYS detoured and blocked, colonial alienation parallelling her own twentieth century equivalent, the I-Lyn Lifshin poems are lessons in stark self-realism, exercises in seeing just what WAY was lost . . . and how.

Marvin Malone's 1977 Wormwood Review "centerbook," PATAGONIA, which I think I should mention here, is almost a DNA replication of LEANING SOUTH—on a much smaller scale. Essentially the same general "mix" as LEANING SOUTH, PATAGONIA begins with an objective Nature-Picture (Darwin Revisited) of Patagonia that begins with The Earth Itself, then introduces Indians, and ends with a cosmic, naturalist's "joke":

> on one beach
> 10,000 cormorants
>
> white throats in
> the sun
>
> only one day
> in the wind
>
> the birds came
> back   seaweed
>
> dripping from their
> mouths to line
>
> a nest and there
> was a huge thud
>
> two birds hit
> midair crashed
>
> flopped over
> twice   dead[19]

The most "successful" part of the "Patagonia" title-poem, though, is a contrast between Nature with Indians and Nature alone, which is the basic thrust/idea-base of the entire poem:

> indians ate the huge
> ground sloths   horses
> an animal that crawled
> along in a shell
>
> the tehuelche boiled
> penguins down for
> oil   when everything

> got used up the
> people went away
> then the seals   sea
> lions and penguins
> came again   every
>
> thing that magellan
> saw in 1590 except
> for the indians[20]

Indians, only not in terms of tribal in-values, but set against the backdrop of cosmic indifference—which is always implied in the Eskimo poems, but never brought out with this dramatic (almost Greek-dramatic!) abruptness.

The "middle-section" of poems in PATAGONIA is all very personal, in fact some of the most personal, painfully personal, poems that Lifshin has ever written.

Put on the Madonna-Mask and then start revealing:

> SHRINKING MADONNA
>
> her skin is so
> delicate you can
> almost see the
> nerve endings
> capillaries
> break down dont
> dream its just
> no vitamin c or
> that she's pull
> ing into her
> self like some
> leaf growing
> backward its the
> incredible shrink
> ing its some
> thing growing turn
> ing to stone the
> dirt on that
> leaf pressed in
> to fossil pressed
> hard and thin
> leaves in a book

> nobody opens
> she's so thin
> when she shaves
> her arm pits the
> hair's too deep
> in to reach
> like her anger[21]

The use of the Madonna-mask enables the "real" Lifshin to step forth. It's the "play" that enables the "essential" to act itself out.

Anger, there's always that base-line, and from it all the negative qualities that only can be admitted under the theatrics of the Madonna-Persona.

The possessive (magnetic) Madonna:

> ....you
> can't resist
> she holds you
> like those
> 12 magnets on
> her old amana[22]

The afraid Madonna, getting a mole sliced off, simultaneously thinking of slicing off her husband/slicing herself out of the "comfort" of marriage:

> ....feels
> the pain lying
> inside her
> tho theyre
> things she
> cant use
> and will be
> better off
> without she
> throws up
> thinking of
> both losses[23]

The conflict here is between what Lifshin *is* and what she feels she *ought to be*—the Goody Little Two-Shoes Syndrome, sugar and spice and everything nice (she's been told), but then she looks into her heart of hearts and finds huge chunks, clouds, deserts of DARKNESS, and the only way she can live with that is to assume the Madonna Pose, put on the mask, and act evil out in very private poem charades.

Which is the why of the third "kind" of poems in PATA-GONIA, the old-house antique "trip" that enables her to substitute for the Self she really doesn't want to find inside her, a whole reality that's detached, distant, almost "scholarly":

> small dark
> room of glass
>
> pewter   dark
> cupboards full of
>
> jars from england
>
> a woman's eyes
> painted on china
>
> glancing down
> looked in
> to the tea leaves
>
> left her name there[24]

And if it's not American old house poems, it's Kyoto ("someone sweeping/leaves with a/new straw broom"[25]) or ("sod houses//no trees the/land hard"[26]) Nebraska or ("geese in the/black holes"[27]) North Dakota, always depersonalization, "objectification," a throwing of Self out of Self into the safe, neutral world of THINGS. In fact aren't all these "objective" poems a kind of private Yoga, Zen meditation-exercises to exorcize the Self and arrive at a plateau of self-less inner-sea CALM? Aren't we being treated to a performance of Zen inner-peace exercises that actually *do* transfer their Zen calm to the reader?

> incense sticks
> in the reeds
>
> huge leaves
> on the water[28]

Isn't the prime purpose of all this multifaceted, multi-identified restlessness an attempt to somehow face up to and live with the Demons she finds inside her. Unlike Richmond she doesn't dwell on and expand the demon-geography inside her; at best she tolerates her Kali-nature. And the "trips" into other "things"/"places" remain alternatives to bring her completely unbourgeois "wildness" stuffed inside a heavy context of bourgeois GUILT.

NOTES

[1] Red Dust, New York.
[2] Ibid., p. 12
[3] "Family," p. 175.
[4] Ibid., p. 174.
[5] Ibid., p. 30.
[6] Ibid., p. 176.
[7] Number 39, p. 47.
[8] Number 7 of "Nantucket" poems, p. 86.
[9] "Falling Thru White Trees, Maine," p. 199.
[10] "Coming Back to Middlebury," p. 196.
[11] Ibid., p. 196.
[12] "The House on North Pleasant," p. 177.
[13] "Howland House" poems, Number 12, p. 126.
[14] "Nantucket" poems, Number 17, p. 96.
[15] Number 38 of Eskimo poems, p. 46.
[16] Number 21 of Eskimo poems, p. 29.
[17] Also from Number 21.
[18] "Fear," p. 206.
[19] Ibid., p. 21.
[20] Ibid., p. 20.
[21] Ibid., pp. 23-24.
[22] Ibid., p. 23.
[23] Ibid., p. 25.
[24] "Middlebury Poems," no. 1, p. 27.
[25] "Kyoto," p. 28.
[26] "Nebraska Then," p. 29.
[27] "North Dakota," p. 29.
[28] "Kyoto," p. 28.

CHAPTER XVIII

There's very little of the existential time-traveller Lifshin in OFFERED BY OWNER (1978). It's a collection that sums up Lifshin as Jewish girl in a gentile world, feeling fat, awkward, out of things; poems about her mother, father, uncles . . . and only at the very end are there a few old-house poems *and* the little explanatory vignettes that retrospectively throw a great deal of light on poetic intentions.

There are some pungent comments on her father, for example:

> Perhaps I've written so many poems about my father because there was so little closeness with him. Sometimes I wonder if it's true, as one psychiatrist told me, that I made him better than he was because I had to. . . .
>
> My mother and I had always been close, I suppose that's why there's so many more poems about my father. . . .[1]

Lifshin follows up this second comment on her father with a very revealing conclusion, that poetry isn't about the known, immediate, explored, familiar, but about the unknown, remote, unexplored, exotic, that poetry serves the poet as some sort of psychic exploration party into uncharted territories, as probes into an unknown that has to *become* known in order for him/her to survive: "If you believe poems are a mask, help show the opposite, something I think is more of a way to understand the poet, rather than trying to pin-point people and dates and towns as if it was history."[2]

If the erotic poems are the result, not of experiential eroticism but rather its lack ("You don't need to write love if you're loving and in love"),[3] then Lifshin's whole emphatic push into the sensory must be because of a similar dialectically opposite need, i.e. a strong psychic bent toward the anti-sensory.

In fact a case could be made for a whole Self-Counterself

theory embodying two polar concepts of Lifshin the Person secreting a kind of Counterself in her work so that the work itself emerges as screen, cloud, mask:

POETIC MASK	THE "REAL" LIFSHIN
Suicidal, introverted, "dissolving."	Life affirmative, extroverted, stabile.
The Loner; recluse.	Gregarious Woman of the Crowd.
Sensualist—Feeler.	Kabbalistic Theoretician—Thinker.

This would negate most of this book, of course, in which I've taken the poetry as (somehow) a projection of The Self. But, nevertheless, there is a whole psychological approach to Lifshin to be explored here in which Reality might be simultaneously Janus-faced, at the same time suicidal and an affirmer of life, inner- and outer-directed, both theoretician and a leaper into the sensual sea. Certainly those little vignettes at the end of OFFERED BY OWNER represent one future exploratory pathway of Lifshin criticism.

OFFERED BY OWNER on the whole, though, is merely another anthological stopping-off place in Lifshin's poetic development and the next major work that flows out of the major current of her evolving development is another Morgan Press book, GLASS, published with an actual piece of glass covering the title.[4]

In some way or other every poem in the volume works out a glass metaphor.

At times glass is the ultimate metaphor of isolation/brittleness/solitude, like in "Wednesday" where the aloneness is further emphasized by a psychotic fragmenting of (aren't they ultimately both the same reality) language *and* point of view:

> plum branches
> don't   even
>
> the glass on the
> quince won't
>
> no cat in
> the windy   no

> the no's like
> a bracelet
>
> ice my
> fingers slip
>
> from i can't
> touch   some
>
> thing between
> me and what
>
> was warm
> burns isolates
>
> like a solid
> glass jumpsuit[5]

Here the universe is a complex of negations. It's as if Lifshin makes a series of small attempts at bridging Negation, reversing polarities, making contact . . . and every time stops short, retreats. Plum branches don't even WHAT? Touch against windows? The cat seems to have been "swept away" by the wind. But she doesn't/can't even know that. "No" rears up; she wears it like jewelry. And then "No" freezes her, touch snuffs out, the formerly "warm" now self-contradicting both burns-isolates and *insulates* "like a solid glass jumpsuit." It's a reality of glass-ice splinters, nothing complete and even the initial curve of contacting is slammed back by the force of a cosmic NO.

On the opposite end of this Everlasting Nay, glass becomes both light-transmitter *and* reflector, an exercise in personal confrontation/honesty:

> the two days i went in
> to town this week i
> bought things that
> reflect the sun what
> ever was light a
> round me   green in
> cense holder   it
> puts the sun on the
> roof of the room
> green green i want
> you i want to see

> you on top like the
> light yesterday i put
> a deposit on a mirror
> bordered by old
> green glass it must
> be the green coming
> thru the window
> green's never been
> a favorite color
> of mine but i
> bought the green
> mirror tho i couldn't
> afford it   you
> might say i was
> finally going to
> look right back at
> what i'd avoided
> the way some
> dreams do[6]

What is it that she's been avoiding *but* light as tool of self-confrontation. The mirror-exercise not only pulls her out of these multiple-pasts that she's been experimenting with (poems as time-machines to explore other lives), but shocks her out of shadows into sun and Nature again . . . the green. Inevitably the green-sun-mirror image-complex brings "company" along with it. The anti-hermit gregarious Lifshin makes a cameo appearance: "i want/you i want to see/you on top." *And* along with this whole thrust toward shared light and sexuality, syntax suddenly comes straight again, the fragmentation is over, we've entered the grammatical order of sanity.

GLASS is essentially a play with the polarities of Light-Dark, Fragmentation-Restoration, Flow-Blockage, Solitude-The Crowd, Asexual Cold and Sexual Heat. It's salvation versus The Lost, sanity versus a total breakdown in psychosyntactical order.

Much of the book is dream/dreamlike/drugstate:

> . . . . the pills nothing's strong enough
> to   i start screaming louder   the
> dead heads   people in the hall,

a poem that ends in the old familiar polar cul de sac:

> ... but there's ice and snow
> slamming all night   each day's
> an iceberg   no one knows
>
> the rest   the terrible cold
> down under   something they
> can't begin to imagine[7]

The drug that keeps reappearing here and elsewhere in Lifshin's work is Ritalin, a Valium-like "calamative":

> Ritalin and rum
> the crushed bar
> berry thru glass
> and thorns milk
> weed stalks like
> small old men[8]

Perhaps Ritalin + alcohol is the trick. It *is* a Van Gogh (his drug was digitalis) hallucinatory universe once it begins to coalesce. The male gets menacingly incarnated out in the fields of milkweed stalks . . . the whole Ritalin-rum "state" seems to be one of rather desperate, violent disintegration:

> even with the pill
> even with so much
> put down on paper
> pods start break
> ing their black
> seeds   o baby i
> know this wouldn't. . . .[9]

And what are we to make of the lines:

> in brooklyn everything
> smelled of cabbages
> and plaster   *at least that
> time they gave me
> morphine.* . . ?[10]

Is there some other unknown drug-input involved here from which this nightmare world is emerging? Is there some "real" connection between the Lifshin hallucenogenic landscape and parallel landscapes in Poe, Kerouac, Burroughs? Or is Lifshin a kind of Blakean "natural" visionary whose highs *and* fragmentations both flow out of an exploratory need to probe all heights and depths, keep "liquid," never solidify in any solid stance or frame of permanent reference?

At any rate what dominates here in the midst of all the variety of experience (and experiments!) is Lifshin somehow fleeing FROM, afraid OF, trapped IN. The dominate glass-ice association is isolated brittleness:

> glass words
> broke in my
> mouth . . .
>
> i expected to
> be that breakable
> growing hard
> something pressed inside
> so long it
> crystalizes
>
> i was waiting for the
> edges to
> crack thru my
> skin[11]

When assuming other personalities, time- and culture-travelling into colonial America, among the Eskimos or other "tribes," she's able to break her own isolation and empathize with both Person and Place. Adapting other Personas is liberation . . . escape. But when reduced back to selfhood (and not time-travelling to her *own* past, other earlier versions of herself) what emerges is The Poet frozen in time, glassed-in from any flexible contact with The Real:

> . . . . you think
> you're going
> under but nothing
> gets thru the glass
> : it's like going
> thru one of those
> automatic   car washes[12]

Only rarely, after a fragmentation-crisis, mental "fog-attack" does Reality weakly shine in, and even then we're closer to the syntax of dreams than waking:

> bells   sun
> on the blue bed
>
> chalk cats lips
> and tulips on
>
> the glass that
> cracks into a
>
> web   new lambs
> in the roses
>
> the poplars
> snowing[13]

The reality of GLASS is the reality of schizophrenic paranoia; we're in the mind-regions of hallucenogenic fear, heightened distancing, numbness, splintered, wounding vision, strangling terror: "the pills nothing's strong enough/to . . . i feel i'm cellophane the same saranwrap. . . ."[14]

GLASS is a classic crackup. There's nothing in Levy or Bukowski, Sexton or anyone else on the "scene" that quite comes to this level of splintering and isolation. In GLASS Lifshin plugs into a whole "other" tradition—Steve Richmond, reaching back through Celine, Baudelaire, Duchasse. Like Richmond's "Gagaku" mad-poems, the work in GLASS is genuinely a reproduction of alternative mind-WORLDS. We are *inside* the battered psyche of the poet; all other (outside) reality disappears and all we're left with is the dream- and hallucenation—furniture of the Mind on the Other Side of the Wall.

LIPS ON THAT BLUE RAIL, Lifshin's *other* 1978 volume,[15] is a funny kind of halfway house that combines the rationalistic sanity and self-awareness of OFFERED BY OWNER and the existential shoot-the-shoots of GLASS.

On one hand, never has Lifshin been nastier:

> . . . . finding most
> people cuckoo or middle
> class   convincing people
> you can do things you'll
> never   throwing your

> name around   wrapping
> yr accent around people
> stocks and bonds locked
> in a house in yr head   i
> saw the family tree you
> sketched in your rug
> book   the good old
> mayflower branches
> still playing poor in a
> dirty loft in soho where
> you cover the walls with
> eggs snear at the houses
> with paintings and pit
> your blue blood at them[16]

On the other hand she's never been more (directly . . . simply) human:

> . . . . I seem to need
> knowing the weekends won't
> be alone or with somone i
> have to decide how to be my
> self with. . . .[17]

There's a kind of frenetic desperation throughout that echoes GLASS, and there's even one poem that's a GLASS escapee:

> light on the ball
> of glass
> on the puddles
> under the Hilton . . .
> a ripple of light
> like a flag of glass
> diamond ripples. . . .[18]

The most remarkable poem in the book, though, is the title poem "Lips on That Blue Rail" that more than any other poem she's written gives us the inside track on the Lifshin creative process:

> i
> decide not to work all
> day lie down on the
> start feeling like

> milkweed let the walls
> become trees   that's
> when it happens   the
> poem like certain men
> like that wild cat who
> won't come when i leave
> it hamburger the poem
>
> thru the leaves   coming
> its mouth on the dark
> like something under
> ground some engine   its
> lips on that blue rail
> color that keeps trains
> moving keeps them strong too

Metaphors mixmaster through multiple transformations, from milkweed, the expanding pod, the *need* for expansion, its natural inevitability, into a transparencing of walls ("let the walls/become trees"), the permeability of Nature, the poem reluctantly, teasingly emerging ("like that wild cat . . ."), displaying its own ("thru the leaves . . .") independent power, its subterranean subconsciousness ("something under/ground . . ."), power again, like an engine . . . and then the most tantalizing image of all—"its/lips on that blue real. . . ," with the surrealistic assertion that its the blue itself "that keeps trains/moving keeps them strong too." The horizontal rail is really vertical isn't it, really is a part of the roadway into the Spirit, and the blue is The Divine and the connection between Poet and Energy is a rail from within the Poet herself to the Sky, again The Transcendental, the nexus with God.

What we're up against here is POSSIBLE LIFSHINS versus THE REAL LIFSHIN, the MIGHT HAVE BEEN versus the IS. Lifshin might have been The Mystic within a viable mystic context, other world, old world, Indian, Jewish . . . Christian. Lifshin *is* the Woman on *this* side of the mystical, confused by the secular and often psychically integrated by the aggregating power of the creative act itself which is a plug into cosmic divinity. LIPS ON THAT BLUE RAIL is one of those little chapbooks written on *this* (secular) side of The Wall.

NOTES

[1] Comment on "Photograph," p. 75.
[2] *Ibid.*, p. 78.
[3] Comment on "The Mother and Daughter Poems," p. 78.
[4] Hey Lady Supplement No. 36, Morgan Press (Milwaukee, 1978).
[5] "Wednesday," again no pagination, poems will be referred to simply by titles.
[6] "Green Glass and Mirror."
[7] Untitled. First line: "i don't recognize an old. . . ."
[8] "The Ritalin and Rum the Old Milkweed Blues."
[9] *Ibid.*
[10] "Cabbages Leaves and Morphine." My italics.
[11] Title poem "Glass" with which the volume opens.
[12] "Oh yes."
[13] "After the Fog."
[14] From the second page of "The I go Down in the Cellar Dream of Dark Snow."
[15] Published by Lion's Breath Press in San Francisco.
[16] No pagination, the title of this poem is "For Someone I couldn't Know Any Better."
[17] "Lately I'm Not Writing Many Love poems."
[18] "Things that Shine in Quebec City as the Sun Falls."

CHAPTER XIX

How different is 35 SUNDAYS from GLASS:

>swallowing too many
>things whole   moon
>rocks in a safe for
>blackmail   he said my
>esophagus was torn
>bones like needles
>my hips look like
>bruised blue plums?[1]

The vision remains "bruised," fragmented, scattered, shattered, and in fact much of 35 SUNDAYS comes off as a kind of "annex" or "suburb" of the larger GLASS-world:

>fish that sleep
>under the ice
>near the house
>
>car lights thru
>the frost glass
>
>applewood burns
>downstairs   i
>
>can't go back
>there again[2]

The line here, though, *is* terser, sparser, more economical. She is paring down, reducing, stripping down to bare minimums. She's come to the point of Maximum Intensity with a Minimum of Words, has become *The* Technician of Contemporary Angst:

>dining room like
>a park unwrapped
>before dawn

> smoke   grey
> mist   a
>
> fly twitching
> in stewed apricots
> giving up   a
>
> boy with nothing
> in his eyes spits
> out a pit as if
> it were his life[3]

In a way what Lifshin is doing here is returning to Meat School as Master Technician; many of the same themes recur— the Male-Female war, isolation, aloneness, nightmare *and* waking violence—but with a finer-honed cutting edge, the Master dallying with the reader, spar-*gaming,* watching to see just what refined twist and lurch of emotion she can manage on the page.

Let's play "drenched," for example, mould-damp, super-saturated moisture:

> raining small motel
> outside varna
>
> my eyes sticking
> together nylon
> sticking to me
>
> strange to wake up in
> a motel like this
>
> smelling water listening. . . .[4]

Or how about Killer, the guy that on Friday tried to steal some bicycles, on Saturday tried to lure a young woman away with him claiming he was a detective, on Sunday:

> . . . . early he
> tied 3 people
> to a tree   stabbed
>
> one over and over
> The shirt is
> his size   what
> the 2 survivors
> remember   is

> as bright as the
> leaves they won't
> stop dreaming[5]

The small poem-scenarios here have an almost expressionistic cinematographic aptness about them, simultaneously well covering surfaces, but also (I'm thinking of Murnau, early Laing) extracting "inner" essences, getting to the cores of small scenes/feelings/"climates."

Lifshin never has been particularly interested in puns and sound-games, but that begins to come in too, like in one of the Sunday poems the gaming with "sloe" and "slow," "need" and "needle," a jazzy, sound-aware riff that "plays" as much as it "reads":

> sloe eyed woman
> getting out of
> bed slow sunday
> woman with the
> mist over a new
> town and the words
> coming thru a
> wall where she
> can't live woman
> you need the needle
> sticks gonna give
> you my way down
> inside if you
> shake for   shaking
> woman   but not
> like in the
> song[6]

She's very aware of this new Jazz-dimension, calls one poem a "Sunday Holiday Blues": "only the small/things are easy/white kittens/curled into/my leg furry/snails//blues i don't/have to practice."[7]

So . . . she's moved into the Annex of the Glass House, dug in and started to hone down, revise, expand techniques, "possibilities." And when she does go *positive,* takes all the fragmentations, rolls them into a big ball and *throws,* it's a whole new kind of power.

Like . . . where else has she ever made a negative-capability, empathetic trip out of, say, *animal* power the way she does in this horse=god=sun poem (section 8 of series "Moving by Touch"), a poem we've already met years before in the volume MOVING BY TOUCH:

> down the coast
>
> drove to see the
> horses leap in
> to the water
>
> black light
> rippling from
> their bodies
>
> what is it they
> smell that
> they plunge in
>
> i watch them
> from a distance
> gripped, my
> face in their
> wet hair
>
> horses coming
> from the other
> side from
> inside
>
> until i'm
> buried in some
> thing they
> are and
>
> sun pulls
> my blood too[8]

The real significance of *this* poem, "capping" as it does, the whole volume, occurs in the words "coming/from the other/side from/inside." It's Lifshinesque empathy not with Past but with very much living Present, and by coupling with the horses here it represents a strong pantheistic urge to dissolve into the All-Present that lies under the surface of the usually fragmented, negative, "downing" Here and Now. This sense of celebration emphatically reaffirms Lifshin's long-present Pantheism which repeated here indicates a new track, life, "escape"—from a surging Now into SOURCES! She's re-found cosmic energy in herself, spliced ("my face in their wet hair") with The Animal in a work that stands next to "Roan Stallion" and "Equus" staring at the incarnation of cosmic awe in (simply) a horse. The fact that it's repeated here in the midst of so much gloom shows just how constant a strain this pantheistic push *is*!

Nor is this poem alone as a witness to transcendental power. Here and there smaller revelations on the same order surge through, a phone off a hook, the cat chasing the sun, coming out of a coma-like sleep and suddenly maples outside:

> like something
> on fire break
>
> ing out of the fog[9]

35 SUNDAYS, then, is paradoxically both a continuation of the crackup aesthetics of GLASS and a bundling together of psychic-forces and sending off on new directions into the immediate, the present, familiar.

There seems to be a straining here toward the decipherment of the hieroglyphics of the everyday, a push away from dream-fragmentation into an unravelling of the mysteries that lie under the unnoticed surfaces of the ordinary. Or . . . is the suspension *between* crackup and revelation a permanent fixture in the Lifshin canon? Already back in 1972 in LADY LYN there was a similar transcendental thrust through surface . . . and never (on the other hand) any definitive break out into any plateau psychology. It's always been the very oscillation between dissolution and reaffirmation that has produced the secret insights and the fresh image-fabric. Perhaps this *is* Lifshin, Menace succeeded by Revelation, and just as reality begins to unpeel and step forth, Menace returns. Perhaps there can't be any stagnation or fixity, and she must remain "waiting for what will/grow to happen,"[10] remain as witness to the dual menacing-comforting flux of necessarily undecodable reality:

> . . . . the room
> full of things
> falling away,
> becoming different.[11]

Lifshin is Levy-like in the power of her visionaryness, but for Levy an entrance into the Kingdom of Vision ultimately meant a tragic isolation inside the Kingdom and an inability to step OUT. Lifshin's very oscillation gives her a flexibility of SURVIVAL!

NOTES

[1] Ommation Press, Offset Offshoot No. 3, Mati No. 14/15 (Chicago, 1979), "The Wind Blowing Thru the Building The Mad Girl's Sunday Fragments," p. 4.
[2] *Ibid.*
[3] "Gould Farm Sunday," p. 27.
[4] "Sunday Almost June," p. 26.
[5] "They Found the Red Shirt Near the Trailer After the Owls Screamed All Night," p. 29.
[6] "Sunday," p. 8.
[7] *Ibid.*, p. 14.
[8] *Ibid.*, p. 40.
[9] "Sunday, Early," p. 5.
[10] "When Are You Going to Move In with Me You Moan in My Hair What About Babies," p. 14.
[11] "The Sheets The Curtain Moving Along the Road," p. 15.

CHAPTER XX

In COLORS IN COOPER BLACK[1] Lifshin finally arrives at the destination she's been travelling toward all along, leaves sweating-self behind, and steps into the role of Pure Buddhistically Calm PERCEPTOR:

> lips   fingers on my
> back pulling   wanting
> to get down what can't
> stay like Monet trapping
> magical colors what
> transformed noon
> something in me is the
> cat tunneling in under
> the quilt over the
> electric blanket making
> a warm sandwich as
> wind blows maples bare[2]

    She's become The Impressionist, true enough, like Monet losing "self" in the sheer virtuosity of trying to capture the evanescent NOW.
    And the book itself comes up to the virtuoso level of this color-capturing, small, hand-stitched (purple thread), the poems are printed in spills and gradations of violets, reds, yellows, oranges, greens, that complement the contents.
    The backbone is taken out of reality here turning it into invertebrate "slime." No defenses, no Self against The Society; no Woman against the Army of Men. The whole book is

> .... like a
> footprint in the
> dunes. . . .[3]

    What the style is really closest to is the work about colonial

American houses, the stack of Old House time-travel meditations—with the noticeable difference that here the negative historical dimension is totally removed. There are no axes to grind, just realities to be entered into for the purpose of extracting "essences."

The "fragmentariness" of Lifshin's vision here experiences a kind of reverse-motion, bringing the fragments of a given reality all together into a split-second's synthesis of "wholeness"/"simultaneousness":

> honey spreads and
> cozes across Monday
> 4 o'clock a slice
> of bread a room
> transformed by
> peace light thru
> old stained glass
> so that the bare
> floors old torn
> rose fading to
> flesh quilt glows[4]

It's as if she's saying "See, my vision never *was* fragmented, what I was really seeing was all the pieces held in a suspension of heightened present-moment awarenessing."

COLORS IN COOPER BLACK is really an experiment in *perception*. This holistic, total-perception that Lifshin is after isn't logical and sequential but anti-logically simultaneous, and the only way WORDS can capture it is by catching all the pieces together in a poem-NET or, using Lifshin's own image, "quilt":

> stained glass marshes
> canadian geese blacken
> the sky   trees heavy
> with yellow apples
> cedar fills with mist
> a woman in a car that
> won't stop wraps in
> words that blur the
> edges she sands the
> days since Wednesday
> smooth as a branch
> sea and wind trans

> form   the words a
> quilt trapping gulls
> pines and the salmon
> sun already sliding
> out of reach[5]

"Orleans" is an interesting poem about writing poetry. The reality outside the poem and the reality of poem-MAKING mesh together, the poet, in fact, both becoming and trapping reality. The edges between the thing MADE and the MAKER are blurred; she has become the things she's writing about, her words both "blur the/edges" and sand them down, ultimately trapping the evanescent Out There before it entirely vanishes ("sun already sliding/out of reach") away.

All along Lifshin has been moving into an expansion of the perceptual NOW, away from Self, the limitations of both personal and historical secularization; here in COLORS IN COOPER BLACK she comes up with an exemplary set of Yogic perceptual exercises:

> amber lights
> asparagus turning
> gold raspberry sun
> sliding into pewter. . . .[6]

For all its shortness (there are only 5 short poems) COLORS represents an apotheosis of the Lifshinian style, a peaking of techniques and directions, a perfection of the Impressionistic Mystique that tries to solidify and fix betraying-Reality in the amber permanence of Art.

NOTES

[1] Morgan Press, 1981.
[2] "Thinking of Yesterday." No pagination.
[3] "Wellfleet."
[4] "Hearing the News."
[5] "Orleans."
[6] "Wellfleet."

CHAPTER XXI

Poetry Now Press's HOTEL LIFSHIN[1] is a good summing-up of the human-side of Lifshin. It's existentially chronological, you go back to a kind of innocence, the "young" perception of The World ("virgin, she/must have been in that/sepia picture/ lace to her teeth/marrying in the old house/a man she couldn't trust"[2]), and end with the jaded, embittered perceptions of the title poem:

>....................... the 23
> men who call on
> the hour couldn't
> much care waiting
> to be picked up
> driven to the dark
> room of her thighs
> like a hairy cave
> no island retreat
> could compare with
> they want food
> they want what
> they want when
> they want it wine
> and hills of skin
> to ski   there's
> just one tip they
> think of and you
> wouldn't really
> say they leave it[3]

You get the overexposed, beleaguered poet here, the Artist in Macho Disneyland, hungered for with a greedy bloodlust that turns her (eternally) back in on her Self. In fact you'd like to have it end on some more positive upbeat than ("Enough"): "Lifshin I say only a/pig would/want it all//the fragments, yes/ enough these//pieces of love,/the words for it."[4]

In general the whole book's an exploration of the Formative Sociology of the (Permanent) Outsider. This is *not* the book of Lifshin the Impressionist, Lifshin the Other-Culture Explorer, the Buddha, the Yogic Master, but familial, being-formed Lifshin exploring the factors and forces that pulled her out of and kept her out of the comforting mantle of the ordinary/"normal"/ expected.

First there's the Chauvisnism, the male-supremacy, the special treatment of The Man:

> . . . when we went to
> visit aunt sophia
>
> she didn't like the way
> we called him ben . . . my
>
> mother grew the chopped
> liver story for years
> on main street   how my
> father's sister treated
>
> him like a king while
> we were starving. . . .[5]

And here in the midst of a chopped-liver poem about the differential (deferential!) treatment of a sister toward her *brother*, another alienating factor emerges, the familial dislike of any sort of "adaptation" to the World of the Goyim:

> . . . . she didn't
> like the christmas
> trees in our head[6]

The System says: the male takes precedence, and you as good Jews forget about the customs/beliefs of all surrounding "tribes."

The psychic escape-route is to dream of being a free Self not trapped in the context of having-to-behave-yourself Christendom. Like in the poem "1918."[7] It's a story of her mother's shoe store, some gypsies come in, everyone's distrustful, Lyn's mother "is dreaming of fires/and tambourines/red skirts swirling" —trapped in middle class commerce the message is FREEDOM IS IN BEING TOTALLY OUTSIDE, NOT BEING AN OUTSIDER

(JEWISH) STILL HANGING ON TO THE INSIDE (CHRISTIAN SOCIETY).

In "You Must Know" there's a key connection between Lifshin's mother's projection out into "gipsiness" and her own journey down the same escapist-path:

> ... by the fifth grade
> i was painting
> gipsies, people
> dancing around
> flames singing.
> the girls had
> straight hair,
> were thin were
> what i thought
> i couldn't be....[8]

She draws gypsies, carnivals, wild horses, always the same escapsit thematic line, the getting out of her own skin *through art,* and then at the end of "You Must Know" comes the revelation:

> ......Later the
> drawings turned
> into words   You
> if you are reading
> this must know
> something about
> want to
> find some place
> outside your life
> where you can
> live differently[9]

A very important fact about the whole Lifshin canon—the poem is almost universally a pushing of the ejection button out of ordinary reality. Which—carried to its ultimate logic—would mean that the "Hotel Lifshin" poems in this volume, the ones that complain about The World knocking at the door, are really a lament about being trapped in the solitary well of loneliness. It's an interesting idea—that the work is always the polar opposite (escape-hatch) of the reality of the person.

There's one brilliant family-portrait poem here that says

volumes about the lack of unity in the Lifshin-world. A photo, "my/mother in front trying to pull everyone/close together for/this photo at least."[10]

The mysterious high-point in the volume (and life?) is "1962 Plymouth," a rich boy whose parents disapprove of Lifshin because of her long hair and nails and black cat:

> . . . . dust rose
> with a top that
> went down with
> a button until
> coming back from
> chinese food in
> a storm   i loved
> the deep squashy
> falling apart
> cushion   warm
> smell of mold
> when i drove to
> meet his bus
> fridays from
> the lake with
> the wind roaring
> i was sure i
> cld go anywhere[11]

The young optimism, feeling of wide-open eternal roads, all-possibility, all-PROBABILITY, the sense of motion, linkage, all part of a windy, billowing-out sense of LOVE, the breaking of solitude. A key-poem that diagnoses the other side of Lifshin's lifelong feeling of separation; here "coupled," in love, loose in an upbeat world, the Curse of the Outsider is cancelled. Only it doesn't last does it. The next poem in the volume is another car-poem, "1969 Healy":

> In boston people
> stopped to see their
> faces in the green
> glow but things
> started breaking
> right away and
> the green rusted[12]

"Up" is very short, however sweet, "down" is the mood of a lifetime.

The mother-poems here aren't new, but placed as they are, in the familial context, one new perception comes through—the relationship is good, intimate, comforting, the problem (if there is a problem) is that the link is *so* intimate that Lyn takes on the coloration of her mother's fears. Like her mother can't light matches, is afraid of fire. It's a shared fear of the Great Menacing Out There. They discover paired-phobias, and after the fire-fear revelation "do you hate to kill flies my/mother asks like columbus/discovering a new continent."[13] Overprotective perhaps, perhaps not, the Mother-Daughter relationship becomes both sadomasochistic and symbiotic, their images reflect back and forth self-duplicating and sometimes becoming confused; who is who, which is which. And perhaps you can say this—the cutting never takes place, the Poet lives forever inside the protective aura of The Great Mother:

> we drive at 3 AM
> slow into Boston and
> strip what looks like
> two clean beds as the
> sky gets light I
>
> smooth on the form
> fitted flower bottom
> she redoes it
>
> She thinks of my life
> as a bed only she
> can make right[14]

In the sequence of the book it's revealing how the Mother-poems are succeeded by a dog (surrogate-baby?) poem and then a Manuscript-poem in which mss. are equated with babies, as if Mother passes to Mothering (the dog) to Mothering (the poetry):

> they're coming back
> in now   they're
> plopping thru the
> mailslot   poor mis
> carried babies....[15]

In fact isn't there a kind of equation that goes Daughter is to Mother as Daughter is to poems, "the/things we can't say/to anybody else."[16] There is that kind of often brutal, always searing honesty throughout Lifshin; the poems *are* her children and between her and her children ther are no rules/walls/holds barred.

There's a stiletto of a poem about people wanting free books but never buying anything, there's the gutting of the middle class in a poem "Reading Tour" ("they are always/apologetic about/kniving in a street/that's not a slum . . ."[17]), . . . and then there's a kind of interlude, unusual, "poetic," "literary" poems, a Daphne-series, woman as green, becoming tree:

>   you know the story of
>   the woman in a
>   turret and how ivy
>   puts its fingers
>   across the moon
>   . . . . I would
>   have lowered my long
>   hair to a lover
>   lured him with blood
>   in a bottle. . . .
>   Only I was outside
>   trying to get in[18]

The mask goes up, the mask comes down, the mask is hard irony, sarcasm, and when it comes down the Lifshin behind it is the soft, vulnerable Outsider again—which is a great strength because by varying between Strong and Weak/El Cid and Alice in Wonderland, she captures all the keys in between, makes herself a much richer, complete artist. Assuming and fixing in any one pose would have been a *usual* limitation that Lifshin escapes from.

Lifshin the Bitch-Goddess becomes the Wood-Sprite, then— suddenly—the defenseless Lover, hyperaesthesically aware of the Nature-/Time-Context around her:

>   wrapping the green tomatoes
>   on the first night the
>   cold was tangible
>   as a cloth. . . .

>   . . . . it
> would take weeks of
> snow with green
> tomatoes frying in
>
> side and the windows
> foggy to know there was
> nothing of summer
> left living
>
> Nights were frozen reeds
> you and I were like a
> river running toward
> what we didnt know[19]

    The sweating, barbed, defensive self disappears and the Poet as Mother (Creator) becomes totally involved with her offspring (poems)—*and not their (or her) relation to the rest of the world.*

    These are the poem-moments of the intensest meditative awareness in which words become mantric evocations to higher states of consciousness/perception:

>   . . . . our skin
> smells of violets
> while they soak
> in the red pan
> overnight till we
> boil them down
> licking the green
> then the pectin
> turns them lilac and
> we pour them into
> glass, amethyst
> sun comes thru
> on the window
> after snow[20]

    Even the IDEA of an amethyst, violet-jelly world takes us out of the shadow-world into the Wallace Stevensish world of pure IDEA. We dually step into the sphere of Pure Essence and (through the looking-glass) the Particular, Individual, Sensory Essences of THE COMMONEST REALITY AROUND US.

Meditation ended more social commentary. Two brilliant, scathing poems on soap operas, a poem on a woman who didn't shit for twenty years, a poem about a little crippled, deformed girl coming in late to a ballet-performance and getting caught in the stagelights . . . the pain goes on, the mordant, clawed, weasel-toothed little poems that mercilessly shred reality, the Vision that takes off all the drapes and veils, gets it down to the bare graveyard BONE, peaking in the poem about the perfect Elaine with the perfect body, the domineering monster who had the world under perfect control:

> . . . . when I
> heard theyd sliced
> the second sweet
> breast away that
> pressed like a nose
> up in the air in
> to piqué cotton,
> I couldn't believe
> anything of yours
> could have grown
> that far from
> your control[21]

Which brings us full circle round, back to the ultimate bitterness (world-rejection) of HOTEL LIFSHIN, Lifshin herself on the edge of FAME. And hating it. The world's misinterpreted the slow, dark eyes looking out of the white blonde face; they haven't been saying "Come on in, I'm open," but "Keep away, I'm engaged in the business of discovering ME." But that's the paradox of the artist isn't it; the explication, concretization, "fixing" of the evanescent, personal, "soft," interior is The Task, and its very accomplishing transforms it into public property, and the public, by definition, remains the most crass, common denominator.

Lifshin voices the monster-reactions in us all, she uncovers the things we don't want to see, the world's prides, rat-foibles, the jock's machoism showing through his pants, the Beauty's perfect body (pride) going lame/cancerous, Mom's pickiness, Dad's distance, all the little peacock prides and vanities of Writers and Editors, the crew inside the "literary game." At the same time the Nepalese Buddha appears now and then and takes us to the edge of the Canyon of Vision and tells us "See!" And we do, we heighten our perceptions of The Mystery, she takes our hands and eyes and guides them along its surface. She's her own paradox too isn't she, the Impressionistic Saint mixed in the same skin with the searing disbelieving irony of a Daumier, Pope, Swift. The greater mystery is, how can so much sensitivity survive under the onslaught of so much (negative) Reality?

NOTES

[1] Eureka, California, 1982, edited by E. V. Griffith. I'm working here from a xerox of the final draft ms.
[2] "Family," p. 1.
[3] "Hotel Lifshin," p. 60.
[4] Ibid., p. 62.
[5] "Chopped Liver," p. 3.
[6] Ibid.,
[7] "1918," p. 2.
[8] "You must Know," p. 4.
[9] Ibid., p. 5.
[10] "Photograph," p. 6.
[11] Ibid., p. 8.
[12] Ibid., p. 9.
[13] "My Mother and the Matches," p. 12.
[14] "My Mother and the Bed," p. 14.
[15] "Manuscripts," p. 17.
[16] "My Mother and I Were," p. 11.
[17] "Reading Tour," p. 21.
[18] "Dream of Ivy," p. 26.
[19] "Other Septembers," p. 34.
[20] "Violet Jelly," p. 35.
[21] "Elaine," p. 55.

CHAPTER XXII

So . . . we move out of the published into the manuscript, to-be-published world . . . possible futures.

An interesting book-in-the-works from BLUE HORSE (Augusta, Georgia) is THE MAD GIRL POEMS in which The Mad Girl becomes a shadow-self Persona that Lifshin "secretes" as a conscious extension of her very un-made inner self. In other words THE MAD GIRL POEMS are in a way an institutionalized permanent mad-girl STANCE; the "Self" remains inviolate, the "Madness" becomes mask, stage-face . . . "role." So, whatever you say about THE MAD GIRL POEMS you're saying about Role, not Person, a definitive split between I, The Essential Lyn Lifshin, and ROLES PLAYED (MAD OR OTHERWISE) IN A MAD (OR OTHERWISE) WORLD.

In "Mad Girl Wishes II," for example, she wants poetry/words/the madgirl-madpoet Persona to explore reality, but wants to step one step short of her previous lack of distinguishing between The Essential (inner, undissectable) and The Role:

> when i put you
> in the poem let
> the poem make
> you real
>
> i want to drift
> into the gone house
> feel the fingers that
> pressed against
>
> the dark pitted
> wood let me
> get into names
> of things i
>
> never touched
> acanthus   dawn

> redwood but
> never let words
>
> stand for the world¹

For years Lifshin has been in the habit of "depersonalizing" ("third-person-izing") heself, but here this sort of objectification becomes not simply a *modus operandi* but permanent set/cast/world-view:

> all thats left
> are the words
> she leaves
> like a trail of
> bread crumbs. . . .²

As permanent, fixed Mad Girl, her perception of her Other Eve Self takes on new starkness and depth. She's a "woman (who) blooms at night. . .," a person who uses her Self as poem-fodder:

> she uses her
> self in poems
> that blow holes
> thru her where
> if you look
> you can see a
> tree with a
> woman pressed
> up against it
> becoming one of
> the branches.³

Here in the Daphne-projection she's never been more strongly Pantheistic, nor has Art (Poetry) had a stronger claim to its separate world-existence:

> words like snow
> freeze along
> that wood, in the
> moon they look
> like petals of
> the weeping tree⁴

She's accepting her laureate (Daphne, after all, becomes a "laurel") role both as permanent and negative with a resigned inevitableness that permanently sets her off, apart, alone.

It's as if up to now she's fought between the monastic isolation of the Poet-Role and immersion in the world, but now she's no longer fighting, in fact pulls the role of isolated poet around her like a shawl against the cold of the world.

Reality becomes seen primarily in terms of "material":

> it's like using
> the hangover to
> make the pain
> worth something...
>
> .... she
> grinds the night
> up fine adds
> her own kind
> of pepper
> now eat[5]

Why plead "Show me how to/keep different//parts of my/ life separate...,"[6] when she's becoming the past master of survival by fragmentation, filled the house with poems, "some with blood/and fat dripping" until Words magically become the only future she has:

> the words become
> a wishbone[7]

She's come to function very effectively on the two levels of Interior (Private) Truth and Social (Public) Adaptability. In one Other Eve poem she gives a remarkable picture of the dynamics of this duality, "pouring coffee ... saying things/that are witty," while the Other Her is acutely aware of psychic-reality "huge/eyes in the/dark house," aware, in fact, of her own "madness" that she manages to keep invisible for everyone else:

> you really can't
> see the paranoia
> bird sleeping
> on her left arm....[8]

Ironically the very splitting here represents at the same time her greatest thrust toward psychological unity and her greatest fragmentation. She functions *in* the world by a purposeful, tactical distancing *from* it.

Moving toward new dimensins of psychological complexity, Lifshin opens doors to all sorts of possible future directions—all deriving from this same split of Lifshin-Poet/Lifshin-Person. In "The Mad Girl Separates Each Room in Her Blood and Dreams of Airmail,." for example, the metaphors become kaballistically involved with the House of the Spirit:

> shuts some parts
> of herself off in
> very small rooms
> they burn to get
> out of. she puts
> that smoke on
> paper. . . .[9]

In other words the hunting-ground, the "lab" becomes a consciously manipulated and studied Self, no longer passively at the mercy of The Out-There, but purposefully concentrating on her own inner dynamics and experimenting with them for the *sake of* her role as Poet-God almost solipsistically involved with her own creation.

We aren't told—staying within the parameters of the same poem—"what kind of person/writes too many/poems above love/ And why those flowers on the walls of the shut rooms move," but this *kind* of Freudian auto-analysis might be one possible way for the poet to move, like Levy (again) in a way, into a hermetic world not of Highs but of psycho-probing and revealing dives into the depths of that one self that contains us all.

Certainly the wound/the tear/the "sickness," won't go away and the problem is to get it to appear:

> If she could just
>
> go around as if
> there wasn't this
>
> torn thing in
> side her   go shopping

> sit in the park
> but it's caught
>
> it's making a hole
> in tuesday   it
>
> won't come up
> or go away[10]

So the "Mad-Girl" poet is permanently wounded—Edmund Wilson's old wound = poet's need for expression theory—and, obviously, as long as there's no way for the wound, the "torn thing," to go away, at least there is a way for it to "come up"/ surface, i.e. EXPRESS ITSELF AS POETRY. Again the metaphor becomes the mansions of the mind—soul, spirit, behavioristic psychological lab-games.

* * * * *

Lifshin has always been "psychological," but in her earliest work it was Bukowskian "psychology externalized," turned out into the sunlight, forced to walk the streets. The early Lifshin canon is filled with the Meat School stance of street-toughness— poetry as street-theatre, avoiding the metaphor of internalized "mind."

The WHY of this meat-stance in WHY IS THE HOUSE DISSOLVING?, of course, is her rejection by Academe and a conscious outsider "posture." In reality extremely bourgeois, protected, outwardly conservative, the Bukowski-Meat School vehicle serves as a means to both dramatize The Inner *and* begin a pilgrimage toward a total metamorphosis of Mind. The House that is dissolving, after all, even here, in spite of all her leaning on "street," is the House of the Mind.

LEAVES AND NIGHT THINGS is the ultimate *negative* limit (short of suicide) in the House of Mind. Filled with death, suffocation, drowning imagery, it shows just how far Lifshin could go before going over the brink, beyond the limit into the zone of no-return as one integral Poet-Person *unit* not distinguishing between herself in terms of Role and Reality. It's poetic-person brinksmanship, a Freudian subconscious creation of night- and death-landscapes that freeze and coagulate in their own cold *Angst.*

One year later (1971), in BLACK APPLES, for all its ties to

LEAVES AND NIGHT THINGS, we strike a new note—real autobiographical foundation-laying in the psychic-mansions. We find out a lot about the WHYS of her impulses and cloud-chamber tracks; she identifies her origins, her Jewish mystical past, and from this "presencing" past she strikes out into a highly sensorial-impressionistic empathetic entrancing into The Now. Poetry becomes a kind of mystical exercise; the divinity in her enters in and takes on the form of the divinity in Nature . . . although still there are strong, continuing overtones of the negative, Kali nightworld of self-destruction. Everything remains "at the still edge of a scream."[1]

In her 1972 volume, LADY LYN, "presencing" becomes all; she takes the impressionistic-mystic dynamic to its logical conclusion (and end). Certainly her most dramatically vivid volume, she almost makes it into a world-view of benign transcendentalism . . . if only she didn't keep coming up face to face with Evil just under the surface of Reality. It's an interesting and necessary stopping-point, a dead-end that she recoils from. That benign mystical thrust that runs all through Romanticism up to the end of the nineteenth century, in Lifshin, as in her existential anti-romantic contemporaries, finds horror on the other side of the mirror.

One anti-Transcendental "flaw"—and the other, an inability(?)/unwillingness(?) to Thoreau-like withdraw from the world into the Peace of Buddhahood.

Lifshin's next volume, a thin poetry pamphlet from Hellric Publications,[12] is more revealing and important that its size may indicate, a long-poem diatribe against one man that becomes a kind of paean against the whole Male Tribe. First begins the by-mail seduction, the sending of Chateau Ausone, the whole upbeat long-distance courtship, and then the appearance—the brutal criminal dishonesty dusted with a certain transcendental sense of idealism:

> . . . . he said how
> we'd live in a
> house of shells in
> the ferns in
> big sur
> high on poems[13]

The Upstate Madonna, one step short of isolated, meditative Buddhahood wants to share it and ends up disillusioned, not just this time but time and time again.

This conflict between the social, shared, communal, community, and the alone, mystical, solitary, individual, between the Poet as Participator in the World and Creator of Worlds, is no place better expressed than in a poem entitled "Alone on a Blanket" that first came out in 1978 and retrospectively can be applied back not only to TENTACLES, LEAVES, but all attempts at "liberation" from the human, although never the existential connection:

> i feel shy un
> sure of myself
> as i was
> 15 i still
> feel my legs
> are too fat tho
> my thighs are
> 19 inches and
> people still
> asked me for my
> i.d.   Blues
> gnaw saturday
> like sand on
> wood tho i
> know
> being over 30
> shouldnt matter
> look men right
> in their eyes
> tho the sun
> glares so
> then i paste
> my books around
> me write notes
> on my skin so
> no one can
> see where i
> am but i feel
> my legs still
> betray me
> Without my own
> man these men

>   with their
>   hard brown legs
>   look like some
>   exotic lobster
>   i'm served ½
>   starved to eat
>   tho i dont know
>   how to crack
>   the shell if its
>   too messy or if
>   i want to....[14]

She becomes The Invisible Woman in the act of writing (writing as escape/withdrawal/security bunker), only her legs (phallic-erotic extensions) betray her *and* without her own secure love-attachment ("without my own man") she remains trapped in the erotic marketplace or, more aptly, the erotic RESTAURANT—after all the image here is men = lobsters she doesn't know how to crack-open/seduce . . . in fact she remains unsure whether she *wants* to. . . .

In other words, Lifshin as Thoreauian recluse never quite makes it into the quietude of Walden; there's always The World, especially the sex-love connection that draws her back into gear/interaction.

MOVING BY TOUCH (also 1972) is a key-volume in the Lifshin canon in that it is the first time that she time- and alternative-culture travels, i.e. escapes the dilemma of in- or out-of-the-worldness as Lifshin by taking on the colors/forms/manners of another society and/or time. She comes to the dead-end realization that within the frame of occidental here-and-now-ness, on the flat plane of occidental one-dimentional existentialism, she is trapped in sex, "movement," the "progress"-centered need to "evolve" totally in TIME. Would Thoreau be able to journey to the Heart of Walden surrounded by the surface-"noise" of The Modern? So she enters—significantly—in this first time-culture trip, into the world of the Amerindian, plunging into the benign heart of reality not as de-tribalized twentieth century woman stripped of her Jewish past, but as Kaballistic-Pantheist who finds an occult link between Judaism and Amerindia.

It's a daring leap out of the American graffiti time-trap, the first of a series of tentative reachings-out into other selves/possibilities, a schizoid splitting necessary to—ultimately—save the integrity of The Self.

In 1972, though, she still hasn't broken "free." Vietnam burns around her and in THE MERCUROCHROME SUN POEMS lacerated American socio-political reality intrudes on the nascent Buddha-reality. It's not just her person/personal-involvement/ eroticism that pulls her into the mechanical Now, but also the intrusive nature of U. S. war-involvement; the national conscience becomes her own. Although, even here, in the midst of heavy military imagery the Indian ideal, escape into the Great Good Place, still appears in a poem like the "Shawnee Idea of Heaven." So . . . even at her most "involved," non-involved detachment still hums like a time-machine just waiting to be really tried and tested.

Which is exactly what MUSEUM (1973) is all about. Here Lifshin escapes from Lifshin, alter-alternative-egos it into possible worlds that have nothing to do with her contemporary U. S. contextual time-frame limitations. Here once and for all she escapes into THE PAST.

And an interesting past it is, too, this first of her many time-machine launchings—directly into the ritualized, sacred-world of the Amerindians. Which also is not happenstance but almost predictable. In Amerindia she finds her own ritualistic "Jewishness" in an earlier, non-capitalist-contexted *purity.* She finds in Amerindia her own religiosity in a "liberated," "unfettered" form. Mainly here Lifshin throws herself into the Amerindian total sense of The Sacred, life unhampered by Time and Capitalism. And of all her various "escapes" into various "pasts," this is her most complete . . . felicitous. It's LIFE TOTALLY LIVED IN THE HUM OF SACREDNESS, EXACTLY WHAT SHE HERSELF HAS BEEN UNABLE TO ACHIEVE IN A CONTEXT OF MODERN CHANGE/"PROGRESS."

Her next time-trip, THE OLD HOUSE ON THE CROTON (1973), for all its excellence as poetry, doesn't have the same aura of mission-successfully-completed about it. Here colonial doesn't spell mystical/sacred, but merely Capitalism shifted back a couple of hundred years. Interestingly enough the same "flaw" in The Contemporary reappears in the colonial—i. e. the dichotomy between The Male (war, destruction, brutality, the tactics and logistics of Death) and the Female (the immediate, the sensory, the life-giving, the existential).

In OLD HOUSE POEMS (1975) the concentration on what she represents as The Female is given even greater scope and sweep. The concentration here is on existentialism "generalized," the all-encompassing (especially female-perceived) sense of TIME. THE OLD HOUSE ON THE CROTON poems are specific "object-journies" into a specific past; the OLD HOUSE POEMS are more a concentration on *the sense of the journey itself*. And in this mode of stress and concentration, Lifshin almost reaches into an equivalent of Amerindian "sacredness" in the time-travelling experience itself. She almost makes it (permanently) into a Walden of her own isolated, meditating MIND!

This whole trajectory into time-travelled Sacredness culminates in a way in the 1975 SHAKER HOUSE POEMS where Lifshin's able to find non-sexual, or perhaps more accurately, post-sexual, sublimated mysticism in the white American past— among the Shakers. The volumes between the OLD HOUSE POEMS and SHAKER HOUSE POEMS (40 DAYS, APPLE NIGHT, UPSTATE MADONNA and PAPER APPLES), although they participate in transcendental time-travel MOMENTS, in the main are a kind of poetic magma welling out of a previous psychological state that should not be allowed to obscure the very clear line of escape from the first Amerindian "projections" into this final "projection" into the Shaker mystique. Expectedly, the SHAKER HOUSE POEMS are also Lifshin's more immediate, "moist," fragile, tactile. The ecstatic sublimated Shaker world is supremely female. With the SHAKER HOUSE POEMS we peak in an intensely concentrated shorthand world of perceptual etudes . . . which Lifshin is able to extend into her next volume, NORTH POEMS (1976), which is Shakerism transferred into the world of the Eskimos. In the Eskimos Lifshin is trying to find the communal, ritualistic Shaker balance in an even *more* perfected form—Man generically tensionless within his own tribalness and in relation to his natural, environmental context.

We're up on a plateau here in both these books. They're experimental models of the sane, ecstatic, humane. Only we're not left there; the time-machine returns to The Now and the next volume, CRAZY ARMS (1977), is an extension of that other Lifshin that flows through 40 DAYS, APPLE NIGHTS, UPSTATE MADONNA and PAPER APPLES: the pathological, trapped, anguished, frozen, tortured . . . sexual.

It's a bipolar Yin Yan back and forthness isn't it, angst to angstlessness, malignant to benign, Hell to Heaven . . . and back again. And perhaps this is the key to the whole Lifshin rhythm, the penduluming between states of ecstasy and despair . . . because her next volume, WOMAN EARLY PLYMOUTH (1977) represents perhaps the furthest reach of the pendulum toward the ecstatic where, in a way, even the Male-Female "war" is forgotten in lieu of A TOTAL ENTRANCE INTO THE REALITY-SOAKING MOMENT:

> snowflowers thru
> the ice   grey
> moss water
> plants   beetles . . .
>
> cat tails and rain
>
> in one room a cloud of
> smoke and roses[15]

In GLASS (1978) and 35 SUNDAYS (1979), almost expectedly we're back on the other end of the pendulum-swing into tortured anguish. But is there a difference, a third-personalization of the Poet into a fractured, tortured Self that has nothing at all to do with the Poet outside the Poetic "Role," so that somehow, the Poetic Self serves as an untouchable Self with no feedback into the Real (permanently distant/concealed) Self? Certainly GLASS, 35 SUNDAYS and the still-to-be-published (by Blue Horse) MAD GIRL POEMS for all their negative polar identity, aren't the same confessional poems as their earlier counterparts. Or are they? To go back to the very beginning, the interviews, didn't Lifshin say that her most shocking, sexual poems were written when she was at her most sexually frozen? Wasn't poetry even at the beginning an alternative-self of sorts, and mightn't even the time-travel poems be considered merely another "version" of a total poetic output in which POETRY IN ITSELF REPRESENTS A FANTASY-PROJECTION OF THE POET AND VARIATIONS AREN'T SO MUCH POLAR OPPOSITES AS SLIGHTLY DIFFERENT CONFIGURATIONS OF THE SAME BASIC FANTASY FUNCTION?

Certainly one thing remains constant and clear—the poet's use of poetry as a vehicle for self-healing. Behind all the masks/avatars/roles the Pilgrim remains constant, trying to find a sane stasis in (or out of) a world that has lost its sense of religious "gleam," its tribalness, respect, rule-system . . . ORDER in which both Male and Female have a place, a *raison d'être*, function. What she confronts is indefiniteness and arbitrariness, what she wants is order pointed toward the maximum realization of the individual breaking the surface-code of reality and entering into the mystery curled waiting within.

NOTES

[1] All pagination from copy of original ms., p. 21.
[2] "A Woman Like This," p. 27.
[3] *Ibid.*
[4] *Ibid.*
[5] "The Mad Girl Cooks Up More Poems Every Night After Dinner," p. 29.
[6] "More Mad Girl Wishes," p. 33.
[7] "Mad Girl on Her Mad Girl Poems," p. 1.
[8] "She Seems Almost Like an OK Person: Or the Mad Girl's Tight Rope in the Trees," p. 3.
[9] *Ibid.*, p. 8.
[10] "Mad Girl's First Day in the Studio Unease," p. 7.
[11] "Hear the Bodies Getting Louder."
[12] Pyramid Pamphlet No. 1, TENTACLES, LEAVES.
[13] Unnumbered pages, the page here begins with "he taught me...."
[14] In NOT GUILTY!, No. 3, February 1978, p. 44.
[15] Two poems juxtaposed, "Snowflowers thru...," and "Cat tails and rain."